HOW TO BE A MOVIE CRITIC

16 CONVERSATIONS WITH CRITICS WHO KNOW

BY

KEVIN SAMPSON

TABLE OF CONTENTS

INTRODUCTION

I guess I'm one of the lucky ones- I've loved film as far back as I can remember. Ever since my childhood, I was always mesmerized by the power of the medium and fascinated with the stories that were told. I just never knew that all those movies I watched, all the *Siskel and Ebert* episodes, and the passionate conversations and debates I'd have after seeing a film was leading me to become a film critic. I mean, can you actually get paid to talk about movies?

Before we get there, think about some of your favorite childhood memories. I'm willing to bet that when it comes to family activities and bonding, going to the movies or watching them at home is somewhere on your list. Over the years, I've interviewed hundreds of people in the film industry, and often ask my infamous question. What's amazing is that when I ask them my question, "When did you first fall in love with film?", their answers almost always involve family. Whether it was a parent taking them to see a certain film, siblings introducing them to movies, or family vacations involving movie marathons, both family and bonding time around a movie is a through-line. What a powerful art form! It's one that brings all forms of art into one, it has the power to unite, and it creates lasting memories in time. Who wouldn't be drawn to wanting to study and talk about cinema? No wonder so many people do it around the world!

Film is a universal language. It has the power to tell the story of who we are as a human race. In fact, if aliens needed to research what and who human beings are without directly interacting with us, they could learn all about us just by watching movies. That may be a weird metaphor, but the truth is that we use film to understand ourselves and to make sense of life. From cautionary tales, to tales of heroism, tales of grief, or tales of the triumph of the human spirit, movies expose and display every facet of who we are.

Now, while movies may be known around the globe, and everyone has an opinion about them, only a few truly speak cinema. The true film critic is one who can help decipher and articulate the film grammar to the general public. Some may deliver a review in which you may have to hold your dictionary close, while others can speak to the layman with ease. No matter what type you get, they can help explain what you might have misunderstood, or even help express your own thoughts in more detail, but most importantly, help you think about the artistry of a film. After all, that's the beauty of learning film criticism-learning the language and skills to view a film as more than just a film. You are learning to see it as a unique work of art and how to analyze it as one might do with Picasso or Van Gogh.

It's my hope that this book will bring insight into the film critic's mind. This collection of interviews with some of the best critics in the business is both entertaining to read and educational. When I first got into film criticism I had no guidance and mentorship in the profession. All I had was a passion for film. So, the seven questions I asked each of the individuals in this book are based out of a need to give guidance to my younger self. I have no doubt in my mind that the answers within will inspire the future film critic and enlighten the current film enthusiast, and will serve as a Delorian for the art of film criticism, giving a glimpse at our past, present, and future.

When I first set out to write this book, I was planning on talking about my early film critic influences before diving into interviews with specific critics based on some recurring themes in their work. Even once I landed on the decision of compiling interviews, I thought I would compartmentalize critics by the medium they notably worked with. Yet, I quickly realized that today's critic crosses the line between most of the categories I would have divided the book by. The game has changed where one isn't just the critic for X newspaper, Y radio station, or Z TV channel. You have to reach people across so many different mediums. So I decided to arrange the interviews by each critic's last name.

I'm so grateful for every person who lent their voice to this book. Their stories are unique but relatable, and they give informational insight as to the struggles and the highs and lows that come with the territory of being a film critic. Their passion is palpable and inspiring, so enjoy it! I hope to see you at the movies! No for real, I want to bump in to you and hear about your journey in film. :)

CHAPTER I

SARAH BUNTING

Name: Sarah Bunting

Medium: Online

Outlet: Tomato Nation (also Previously.TV, Indiewire, MSNBC.com and others)

Years active: 22

Top 3 movies: *Goodfellas, Diner, Ocean's 11*

Favorite Director: Francois Truffaut

Sarah D. Bunting, also known online as Sars, is an American blogger and journalist and the co-founder of Television Without Pity (TWoP). She has written for a number of magazines and journals, and has received recognition for her website, Tomato Nation, which features a mixture of film, TV and sports content.

Some people have a way with words. As a critic, that can be extremely helpful, not only in separating you from other critics, but by being a refreshing voice for your followers. In addition to having a way with words, Sarah has a sense of humor to match. This humor is evident in her writing and it's easy to see how she blends in witty critiques with a touch of funny. Who doesn't want to have a laugh while seeking to understand what the latest film or a certain TV episode was about? Yet, Sarah uses a certain level of vulnerability and honesty in her work that makes her writing not only enjoyable but relatable. That's a great balance that is such a difficult skill to master.

Kevin: Sarah, first question is when did you first fall in love with film?

Bunting: That was a tough one. I stared at that one, like, "I don't know." I'm not sure I fell in love with it so much as I clung like a life raft, there have been – I have anxiety disorder and as far back as I can remember I've had it. And as an adult, before I finally got on a prescription that helped with it in a real way, there were a lot of life hacks that I was using to chill and get myself to sleep. There were certain movies that definitely were that life raft for me just being able to put them in the VCR – that's how old I am – and [I would] just be lulled to sleep by this familiarity of them, or taken to another world with a different group of people and being able to step out of my own life.

So, that's not really – that's more of a codependent relationship than actual love.

[laughter]

But I will say I used to – I wasn't big into babysitting as a teenager, but I did occasionally do it for family friends who had kids my younger brother's age, so it was like they would be there anyway. And our friends, the Konin's, had this one particular video tape – again I'm from the era where every family had those super long play, VHS tapes that they crammed a bunch of movies on that they taped off of TV.

Kevin: Right. The eight-hour ones?

Bunting: Yeah. [Laughter] So, you could get three movies on

there. The Konin's had one that I ended up borrowing, and I think I still have it. I think it's still in my current house somewhere. It had three movies on it. I don't remember the middle one, but the first one was Breaking Away, and the last one was Diner. I always just skipped over that movie in the middle I guess, and I mean, I'll try to dig out the tape because now I'm curious for myself.

But I quote both of these movies constantly, I think only people who know both the movies well even realize that I'm doing it, but a lot of my daily dialogue is actually Barry Levinson. Those movies are for aspirational camaraderie that was missing in my own teenage life. It also felt real, and disbelief was easy to spend with those movies. So the creation or the recreation of another world that I could just step out of my own life and into for a couple of hours has always been something that I needed and have been grateful to filmmakers for.

So, the short answer is mid '80s is when I fell in love with film. My parents weren't big film buffs, so it wasn't that sort of growing up experience that I had, but I would say discovering most movies and how they could take me out of some unpleasant times in my own life. It was definitely key.

Kevin: What drew you to the art of film criticism?

Bunting: Well, it was the '90s and everyone had their web journal, and you had to write somethin'. [Laughter] I mean, the thing is – I don't mean to be flip about it – but occasionally I am also asked why I "chose" to become a writer, and it's like if you can choose to do that, choose something else. [Laughter]

Kevin: Right.

Bunting: It's like, no way for a grown up to make a living.

So I didn't exactly choose it, it's just something I had a reasonable facility with doing. And nobody was asking me to be an umpire!That's as far as writing goes. As far as being a critic goes, like I'm primarily a TV critic – I think if you go on my Wikipedia page, that's the lead. But criticism of any kind was sort of drawn to because I've always been kind of that role in a classroom, the sarcastic commentary person.

But then on another level– if a film is working, or if it isn't, why is that? Like, I just like to look at it and analyze it for myself. Then, if you have a blog and you post reviews, and people commenting on it then you know you're sort of investigating it together. So, I guess that's what drew me to it, this interest in why a story is or is not working. And then the ability, if it really wasn't working, to make cheap jokes at its expense was also appealing.

Kevin: I love it. All right. So, if you could, you know you founded Tomato Nation in '97, correct?

Bunting: Yeah, end of '96, '97. Oof!

[Laughter]

Kevin: Yeah, so...

Bunting: It's been a few Presidents now, yeah.

Kevin: [Laughter] Nice. So, if you could, how did you find your voice as a critic? So, even with what you just said, in terms of analyzing why a story worked or it didn't, but then also as you said just coming up with some quick joke. Even when you read on your website, you can hear your voice coming through. So, for the critic or up and coming movie review that's trying to find their own voice and be uniquely

themselves, how did you do that?

Bunting: To tell you God's honest, I'm really not sure. I think the trick is to not try to have a voice TM and not to try to have a brand right off the bat. I think you have just to try to respond honestly to what is in front of you on screen. I mean, like I said, I'm mostly a TV critic and I started out with that, doing recaps of Dawson's Creek, and some of that early work which, you know – it takes some digging in the way back machine to find it, which I try not to do, because it is really strained and trying real hard to be arch and superior and over-swinging at every pitch, so to say.

As time went on, and I watched more stuff and learned more about what goes into making a visual narrative. I was low level crew on a few friends' projects. I read this quote from Vince Gilligan, who created Breaking Bad, that even the crappiest movie or TV episode was "miserably hard to make". So, you go on in your life and you try to have some compassion for the process and also do not go quite so hard at people's physical appearances – like a kind of young, dicky, easy thing to do. You're not pulling punches, you're just keeping in mind that, you know, these things are made by human beings and not everyone is good at everything, every minute of the day.

I guess just doing it a lot for a while. That's not what anyone really wants to hear but it's, you know – you just got to practice. And the voice will come on its own, eventually. There's this writer Bill James who is like the godfather of Sabermetrics and also a true crime writer in the last few years, who has said he doesn't consider himself a writer. He's just telling you what he finds with his analytics and his research.

So, as a result, he is very direct and unadorned and doesn't do a bunch of the writerly, creative writing major bullcrap that I am certainly guilty of [Laughter] still sometimes. He's just not trying too hard and he's communicating the information in a fairly stripped down way that gives it its own poetry. Like, just tell us what happened like it's a conversation, and I think that's what most people respond to with writers and critics that they enjoy and that they look to talk to them about what we are seeing, not tell them what to see, but more, "This is how I'm responding to it and here's that context for it" and so on and so forth.

So, I think that we live in a world, here in 2018, where jokes – jokes about having a brand are not jokes anymore. I feel like everybody has to have a brand. Like my husband and I joke about it with our cats. If the one cat that has kind of an Eeyore personality is being feisty and pouncing on a cat toy, we're like, "That's totally off brand for Pearl." I mean this is the world we live in – it's very important to be able to elevator pitch whatever you're doing. That is important and that's just the world – you have to adapt. But I think if you try too hard to have a voice– it's like "Don't think about an elephant" kind of thing – you have just to write the criticism.

You have to watch the thing, think about the thing, write down what you thought about the thing. Then your own rhythms of speaking and if you're someone who puts jokes in, then you put jokes in. I think it's a mistake if you're starting out to be like "I need this joke ratio". You just have to do it for a while, unfortunately, there's no magic bullet. Or, there wasn't for me, maybe some people just spring fully formed from their own heads – but not this guy.

Kevin: Yeah no, you gave some golden nuggets right

there.

[Laughter]

Kevin: You did, you did. [Laughter]

Bunting: I try.

Kevin: [Laughter] All right. So, if it's true that there are only seven basic plots in the world, how do you keep a fresh eye for every movie or a TV show that you watch?

Bunting: It's worth noting up top that we don't always get this right, [Chuckle] frankly.

Kevin: That's true.

Bunting: I can think of a few reviews by the late Roger Ebert who is sort of the gold standard of criticism. And I believe he did try to go to everything fresh and he considered that very important – you can't expect Transformers 4 to be Day for Night or whatever. But he had few pieces that sort of put me back in my chair – that he was not responding necessarily to what was actually happening. The one I'm thinking of is his review of Zoolander, which I could act out that entire movie from memory.

[Laughter]

Bunting: I love it. But it came out in October of 2001 and there were people having a lot of PTSD reactions to things that on the surface had nothing to do with what was in front of them. And that happens, you know, like I said before, movies are made by people and they're reviewed by humans, also. So you never really know what's going on with people who you don't live with, right?

There are only seven stories, but it's also possible once

you've been watching movies and watching TV for any length of time, you know how many variations there are, – bad and good – but it is possible to route them differently to the conclusion that you know is coming, or to invert the tropes that are there or even just tell whichever plot it is. Like plot number four, but the actors are very appealing and have good chemistry with each other, and then you're just in and out of it in 89 minutes. There is an elegance to not trying to reinvent these things.

See my previous comments about things being miserably hard to make. Sometimes a movie is just not conceived correctly. And overall, it's not going to work but it can still do interesting things and be entertaining in terms of autopsying it after or being like, "Well, why didn't this work?" Sometimes Keanu is not cast in his strengths, but he's always really trying very hard to do whatever it is he's doing and that's worth something.

Or, you know I don't like musicals – that's just something that I say about myself – but I can give you eight paragraphs on West Side Story, no problem. So, I guess the short version of that is that you just try not to think about that. There's nothing new under the sun, well, you know [Chuckle] the current political situation in this country suggests that maybe things that we've never experienced before are not to be desired. And I'll just leave it at that.

So yeah, you have to just try to let things, – performances and stories – be what they are and not to expect them to do things they didn't set out to do. And you can also see the only seven-basic-plots thing as a positive – that it's a way of organizing the world. That's how storytelling is, really. So, the fact that there are only seven of them organizes my world as a critic just like "Which one is this going to be? Oh, number five. All right, let's see where it goes."

Kevin: Right, right. OK. So, what advice would you give the up-and-coming critic or movie reviewer?

Bunting: Go to law school – all right, mostly kidding. But actually, low-key that will focus your writing and your ability to process huge amounts of information and synthesize them rapidly. So, I guess that wouldn't be unhelpful, just a little expensive for most people. But seriously, this is the same advice that I would give for any writer which is: consume as much story as you possibly can to develop your ear for it. Andy Warhol – or actually it was Bob Colacello who was writing about Andy Warhol – once said that "you can't send up what you don't have down". So, having the grounding in all kinds of narrative so that you know how it normally behaves is key and it's also fun. There is nothing better for your small talk game than being a TV critic, nothing. Unless you're a sports writer I guess.

So, I would say, watch movies, TV shows, even reality shows, those that have a build and you should know how it's done. Read books and magazines and tiny letters and listen to podcasts and hip hop, and podcasts about hip hop. All media is storytelling, basically. This is like a primal Homeric need, like I said before, to order the world by retelling it as it were. If you immerse yourself in all kinds of stories then you're better able and confident in looking at it, and either diagnosing it or describing it in a way that is useful to others, if that's the kind of criticism that you do.

My thoughts on The Post are maybe not groundbreaking, but I came into that movie with everything that I already knew about

Tom Hanks from seeing Big 88 times. And everything I know about Meryl Streep from seeing Sophie's Choice 12 times, everything I know about Spielberg– that super off-putting memoir of Ben Bradlee that I've read grudgingly. Just living and listening to music and all of it. And also, reading other critics and if something that they write or say affects you, just make a note of what it was, and how it was done because that's what we're – I think that's my job – to start or continue a conversation about the work.

So, if it's just a sort of service piece that 's like, "This is the plot, and if you like X-film then you'll like this three quarters as much." That's one thing. But, in an analysis, if you're reading something that's an asinine-like comment and you're reacting really strongly to it in whichever way that's useful to understand like, "Am I upset because the critic disagreed? Was this phrased in a way that was off-putting? Or, is this getting at something deeper and more uncomfortable in the culture that is reflected in this film?", for example.

So, consume as much story as you possibly can, all the time. Like, even in the shower, have a podcast on. Put the phone on the back of a toilet, you know, [Laughter] it's useful, and you don't even realize it's useful – but my parents did not let me watch TV when I was a kid, except nature shows and PBS. If I wanted to watch something else, I had to go through committee and – Dukes of Hazzard was shot down and I'm still mad. That show is horrible – my dad was like, "I am dumber from watching this to see if it was suitable for you. It isn't. Go read a book." So I did, and I was reading and I still love to read – not that anyone has time anymore. But I mean that's the trick if you want to do any kind of – writing whether it's creating your own stories or reacting to other people – you have to just be immersed in how it's made.

Kevin: Yeah, it's interesting that you said that because that's a good point. One of the things I always do and I've been doing since way back in early 2000s, I was listening to Filmspotting, or different podcasts and at the time I didn't realize that one day "You'll be a radio host then you'll have your own podcast." But it all helped me, even in terms of film analysis but also how I am as a host, some of the ways that Elvis Mitchell just transitions but recalls things that he said in his conversation helps. So, to your point, I just think that that's brilliant advice.

Bunting: Yeah.

Kevin: Last two–

Bunting: And one more thing, it's not for nothing, but when you get those freelance jobs, and you have, editors to work with, they're going to boil your beautiful complex grand theory of the Star Wars prequels into a quick baby headline. That's just life. Everyone has their jobs to do in this business we call show. So, [Laughter] just try to accept that in whatever medium you're working in – especially if it's the internet and it's a click or SEO-driven situation. It just is.

It doesn't mean that your beautiful textured insights won't be appreciated by someone. It's just not going to be in the headline, and that's life. And accept it now [Laughter] that you'll have headlines put on your shit that you're like, "Oh my God. [Laughter] That was not me!" Like everyone knows, it's okay.

Kevin: Right. So, last two questions. The first one is why is the film critic important? Or, on the flip-side, is a film critic important?

Bunting: Well, yeah. Important is not a word that I'm super comfortable with, but I think that criticism – at least in my corner of the internet – and responding to and talking about TV and movies was like the internet, at least where I started out. So, important, I don't know, but I think critics definitely have a function.

Art is never about only what it's about, if that makes any sense. Even sports are never only exactly about whatever game is being played. Like, I'm a huge baseball fan and as with many games, the dramatic narrative is based right into it from the get. Like, there's The Hero's Journey, there's the triumph over evil, triumph over adversity, blah, blah, blah. And whatever work of art is a way for the artist to receive and process the world and reflect on the world. In the same way, the criticism is a way for the audience to do the same.

So on the one hand, you have the role of criticism as – like I said before – more to service the "If you liked All the President's Men, then you'll like the The Parallax View" kind of thing. And learning from your favorite critics, like how they tend to think, and what they tend to like. And you can use that as a parameter for yourself. On Tomato Nation, I've done a series a couple of times with my great good friend and colleague, John Ramos, 31 films in 31 days– do not try this at home.

I wanted to partner with him on it, because we do have similar tastes but also when we diverge, he's absolutely reliable like, "You, Sarah, will hate this, don't pay for it in the theater" kind of thing because we've known each other since I was a child. And we've been working together on writing stuff almost as long. So, that's very useful. There's that service aspect to what critics do, but it's also about getting into a conversation with and about, not only that movie itself, but the artist and the audience.

Maybe not Marvel blockbusters but even those a critic can talk about "Why are we responding to this franchise at this time in human history? What does it tell us about ourselves? Is it trying to tell us something about ourselves? What is the context of that which a non-critic who's reading or listening might not have in his or her job?" – that they might not know that sort of context of the history of horror movies and the history of depictions of African-Americans in Vaudeville that all kind of come together in a film, like Get Out, that you as the critic are able to provide a little more footnoting for that conversation.

So, critics can start or guide a larger cultural conversation about what a work is "really" about, and give some historical context and then sort of see where it goes. Which I think is not important in the sense of "VIP important" but I think it's something that humans need. And we get to watch a lot of movies while we're doing it, so it's not the worst job. It has pain but – [Laughter]

Kevin: Yeah.

Bunting; But yeah, it's like our seminal thoughts on – like I'm just someone who wanted to live right off the cable bill. [Laughter] Who am I? But I have been doing this for a while and occasionally I come up with an insight about something, or can get a conversation going about stuff. I think everybody always lives in trying times and if you'd rather just take a break and think about the larger meaning of the failure of The Real Housewives of Miami – I mean no one wants to do that except me, but if there is another person, call me, let's see a way.

Kevin: Awesome.

Bunting: So, it's a way of making connections, I guess. Not to be too grand about it. My degree is not in Sociology so I mean I don't know, I'm not making things up but, some of my grand theories are just theories.

Kevin: All right. Well, last question is where do you see film criticism is heading?

Bunting: You are talking to someone who is like, "A video iPod? No one is going to buy that horse shit." So, I am really not good at conceptualizing things that don't exist yet – this is a thing that my family has noticed. My brother came over one time and I had rearranged my living room, and I was about to do it the third time as he was standing there. He realized that I basically have a processing delay. I can't just imagine where things are going to go. I have to see them there and then decide. So, it's hard for me to see even a couple of miles ahead. But, I certainly never thought – now I have all these podcasts and I don't do as much, just pure text writing. It's the same basic skill set but it's also a lot different and I had to teach myself to edit podcasts, and I didn't see that coming. I'm not unhappy about it.

So, with that boulder of salt, I think that criticism might get more tailored maybe or bespoke, not necessarily in a bad way just extremely micro-targeted with – the algorithms exist to do this. And eventually I think we will live in a world where you can ask Alexa to brief you on "Which Netflix documentary from Europe should we watch?", and then Alexa will sort of pull critics that you tend to gravitate towards on Rotten Tomatoes. Or, a podcast that you tend to listen to and Alexa or Siri or whatever intelligence is at work at that time, will start pulling extremely tailored information and then you can even select who's going to be rating it. Like "What voice will this come to me in?" And then Benedict Cumberbatch will just read this whole paragraph that Alexa pulled together or that Benedict Cumberbatch will do it, I'm sure we are not far away from this.

So, I think that that's going to be the future of it, but I'm not sure that on the creation side that we're going to see much difference because we've also been hearing "Well, this is it for magazines!" and they're still hanging on. Whether they "should be", but the brave new world of everybody just having a port in our necks is not here yet, and I don't think – except for that hardware – that it'll look a lot different in terms of choice.

Because, in the past, people trying to predict what's going to happen – at least in terms of how content is consumed – always tend to think that people just want a menu and then they want the menu to pick everything for them and that's not exactly how it works. You saw this with – everything was bite size, and then it was the return of long reads – we used to just call this an article. Why do we have a new term for – #longread, like OK, it's just a piece that – I mean we didn't need a new name for it. Anyway, I'm really not sure. This old lady is still like, "YouTube stars, are we still pretending that's a thing?" That is a legit thing, those people make so much more money than I do.

Kevin: Oh yeah, they do.

Bunting: I should really stop talking shit – like I'll be a YouTube star, does the cat food company want to sponsor my super glamorous lifestyle that's covered with lint? Who doesn't want to watch that on their phones? So yeah, I'm really not sure, but I think attempts will be made to customize the voice prompt search experience using criticism and there's going to be some growing pains with that like there always are. I mean [Chuckle] some of the things I used to work on that never got out of beta – like I was the CD-ROM Content Editor, I actually have to explain to people under 25 years old.

Kevin: Right.

Bunting: It was like a DVD and they thought that that was going to – it was that versus the internet. And everybody was like, "Don't bet the internet." Oops. [Laughter] So yeah, it's hard to say but I think that criticism in the main– like how it's written, and what it does for people has not really changed that much. There have been some delivery and distribution changes but I think the future of criticism is probably more or less the same as the past. Hopefully a close eye on and commitment to diversity of voice and experience– that's always welcome. So that it's not just a bunch of white dudes and Pauline Kael anymore, but there's still work to do on that.

Kevin: Right.

Bunting: And on making this a priority in public education and stuff like that. I mean don't bet that prediction because making anything a priority in public education, good luck! [Laughter] So yeah, that's my spiel.

CHAPTER 2

ARCH CAMPBELL

Name: Arch Campbell

Medium: Print, Radio, Television, New Media

Outlet: NBC, WJLA TV

Years active: 40+

Top 3 movies: Casablanca, Vertigo, Being There

Favorite Director: Quentin Tarantino

Arch Campbell has reported on movies, theaters, and entertainment in Washington, D.C. as well as nationally since the 1970s. The Washington Post calls him a local legend. His career includes 32 years at NBC and NBC for Television as well as 8 years with WJLA TV News and its sister station, News Channel 8.

His movie and entertainment reports continue as he is the co-host of At the Movies with Arch and Ann, a weekly podcast with Washington Post lead film critic, Ann Hornaday. When I first moved into the DC area in 2008, I went to grad school, studied film, and eventually I started my journey in becoming a film critic. Along the way, Arch Campbell was the guy that everybody always talked about. If you're in the DC area, Arch Campbell is definitely the name of a longstanding staple in film criticism. If you've ever had the pleasure of sitting next to Arch during a movie, you'll quickly find that he has tons of quips and jokes that he doesn't mind sharing with you or the screen. His laugh is instantly recognizable and he's the same person you see on TV or hear on his podcast. You don't last in the business for over three decades without doing something right!

Kevin: Arch, I really appreciate you talking with me about film criticism, your career, and the future of this medium that we love.

Campbell: Well, thanks for asking me.

Kevin: The first question I wanted to ask you is: when did you first fall in love with film?

Campbell: Well, I think I really got interested in movies when I was about 12 because when I was growing up, Shock Theater came on in my local hometown of San Antonio, Texas. My father had loved movies because he grew up – or really came of age – in the 1930s when movies were so important. So the series started in the late '50s with a host, "Now, let's go to the laboratory for tonight's Shock Theater."

They showed the Universal classic series from the '30s. They showed Frankenstein and then Dracula and then The Mummy, The Wolfman, the Invisible Man, all those classics that my father had seen when he was a young man in his 20s. And that's when I first got interested in movies. Shock Theater and also the fact that because I grew up in the '50s with television, in the '50s, TV was considered the enemy by motion picture companies. So they came to an arrangement that television would not show films made after 1948. So because television in the '50s was like your iPhone is today.

[Laughter]

I mean it was this marvelous technology. Just the fact that you got a picture was thrilling. And the stations used a lot of film because they had to fill in their broadcast day. So I saw all these great movies from the '30s and '40s, Casablanca, the Frank Capra films, Grand Hotel, and I was just steeped in classics as a kid. But basically, I would say the thing that really grabbed me was Shock Theater. Since then, one of my best friends in town is a guy named Dick Dyszel who hosted Creature Feature on Channel 20 in the '70s and he still does screenings at the AFI and they will pull up some film. He showed Frankenstein. He showed other stuff. And he is always nice to invite me to come up there and talk about the great old days with movies.

So the short answer to your question is: when I was a kid and when they started showing horror films on Friday night.

Kevin: Yeah. That answer kind of reminds me when I was younger, I was in elementary school and my fascination with the movies, there was this book called Lon Chaney the Man of a Thousand Faces.

Campbell: Right.

Kevin: And that book to me, I was just in awe of how one person could have so many different faces in the movies and acting. And so, as you are talking about Frankenstein, I remember seeing even those images in books as a kid and I think that – one other thing that you're kind of mentioning is the black and white, right?

Campbell: Right.

Kevin: When the medium was fresh and kind of had just

started, you didn't have the opportunity to just shoot as much as you want. You had to tell a concise story. It had to be framed right. It's something beautiful about those older films.

Campbell: Yeah, because they were inventing the form as they went along.

Kevin: Yeah, exactly. All right. So the next question I wanted to ask is: what drew you to the art of film criticism? I know you have talked about yourself as the accidental critic. So maybe you can kind of give us how you got into film criticism as your career. I think there is an art to being a film critic and I will kind of get into voice later, but what drew you to the art of film criticism?

Campbell: Okay. I'm going to give you the long version of being a critic. [Laughter] Basically when I was growing up, my dream was to become a pianist. I wanted to be a piano player. My father is a great influence in my life and he had a lot of talents including the ability to play piano by ear. He was a self-taught pianist. And he was kind of a restless soul. He never slept so he would stay up all night and he would play the piano and I'd hear him in my sleep. I wanted to play piano like him, but my parents weren't able to afford piano lessons until I was about 14 years old.

So when I was 14, I took first year of piano. At the end of the season, the teacher said, "OK, we're going to have a recital and you'll play your pieces in recital." I show up all proud and ready to go. And I realized that at 14, I'm in a group with a bunch of first graders. And there I was with thick glasses, fat, total loser, and it embarrassed me so much that I quit. I quit taking lessons. So I gave up on my piano playing dream.

Then in high school, we get to choose an elective. For a little while I was in the band but I found that I really didn't have any talent for music. So I decided I wanted to become a photographer and I signed up for Yearbook and I worked in the photography lab at the high school. One afternoon, a photographer and I decided to roam the campus and look for interesting shots because we would expose film, take shots, and develop it in the lab. We had [something] like a photography candy store.

So we're walking around the campus and the Vice Principal sees us, "What are you boys doing?" [Laughter] "Oh, we're taking shots for our photograph lab." He says, "Well, where is your hall pass?" And of course, we didn't have a hall pass. So the yearbook sponsor kicked me out of the photography department because she was embarrassed. So that ended my photography thing.

Finally as a senior in high school, I took a speech class and I seemed to thrive in that speech class and the teacher took an interest in me. Me and another guy decided we would enter the talent show and deliver a 2-man comedy routine. And the speech teacher had encouraged us to do this. There was a drama teacher who sponsored the talent show. Afterwards, she came up to me and my friend and said, "Boys, you two stink! [Laughter] You're not going to be in my talent show."

But then she turned to me and she said, "But you, I want you to emcee." So my speech teacher turned me over to this drama teacher and we would get together every morning in first period and we started writing the script for the talent show. With me and the teacher and about six other people – I was 17 years old, it was like being a grown up. We were tossing ideas around and then she had her typewriter there. She'd bang them down and put them into the script and I really participated in that. I thought, "Well, this is for me." And I went out and appeared on stage and told a couple of jokes and the audience just screamed, [Laughter] partly because they were out of class but also because there I was suddenly performing.

After that day, it changed my position in the school. Suddenly, I was known. And I thought, "Well, this is what I want to do. I want to perform." The drama teacher left the high school I went to at the end of that season, that semester. When I graduated, she moved to a community college and started a radio television program. So I went with her. I decided I would study radio because both she and the speech teacher said, "You have to go into broadcasting. You have a good voice and we'll work with you and your accent." I grew up in San Antonio, Texas and still, every now and then, I could hear a little trace of the Texas accent.

So I followed her to this community college. She started teaching radio. In my sophomore year, I became her teaching assistant. She put up an FM radio station on the air at that school which is now one of the best regarded radio stations in San Antonio. One thing led to another and I went off to the University of Texas at Austin. I got a job in a radio station and I kept working in radio stations. Because I had a good job, I stayed and I got a Master's Degree in Journalism because I thought that this is the path for me. I'll work in radio and then I'll go back and I'll teach at that community college with the teacher who helped me so much. She had told me, "Get your Masters, come back and I'll get you a job teaching."

Well, in the meantime, I got a job at a bigger radio station in Dallas and they had a television station. And their TV news department was expanding every year. And their license was challenged. Somehow, they found that I had a Master's Degree in Journalism so they said, "We want you to do research on this station for our presentation to the SEC to get our license renewed. And then after that, we'll put you in the news department."

So I switched from radio to doing this research project and then I went into the newsroom and I wrote, copied, and produced the newscast. I wanted to be on the air because I've been on the air and radio for 5 or 6 years by then. I started doing feature stories that were non-dated and they liked my stories. So I sort of did feature stories for the local television news. And this was in the early 1970s. You have to remember, I'm old as hell. [Laughter] All this happened 40 or 50 years ago. I'm about to be 72 years old.

Kevin: Wow!

Campbell: So I mean this goes way back. In the early '70s, television news suddenly came into its own and television stations suddenly focused on their local newscast. That's when eyewitness news and all this stuff came along. I became the feature reporter for a pretty well-regarded TV station in Dallas. And they went through some upheaval and a new news director came from New York to run the station in Dallas. He was quite boisterous and would storm into the newsroom every morning and start screaming at us and giving us assignments.

One day he came in and said, "I want a movie reviewer. Who wants to do it?" And because I had grown up with coaching from my father who when I was a kid, he would say, "I watched this movie when I was your age and it's coming on TV. You may want to watch it." And when I sat down in front of the TV every night at 10:30 on Friday to watch horror movies, the horror classics, I raised my hand. I said, "Well, I want to do it." He said, "OK. You're the movie reviewer."

So that week, American Graffiti opened. I went to a screening and I went on the air and did a review of it and they liked it. Now, here's the thing, by the time the guy came and said, "I want a movie reviewer. Who wants to do it?" I've been working in TV news for about 2 or 3 years, so I knew how to write for television. I knew that you needed a plan to review movies. So right then, I decided I want people to know what I think when I'm finished.

I'll give each movie a 1, 2, 3, or 4-star rating. I'll summarize the plot. I'll pitch to a clip. I'll give a reason for why I liked something or why I didn't like something and then I will reinforce it with a rating. And somehow, I knew to do that. I don't know if I learned within a class in college or just what. But that's my story. I was in a newsroom. Somebody said, "Who wants to be the movie reviewer?" I said, "I'll do it." And when I got the opportunity, I put together a plan to make it work. I went on the air and it worked.

And so, I was working in that station in Dallas and really loved working. I never particularly wanted to leave. A guy had left and gone to work for NBC in LA and he recommended me to a guy coming from LA to Washington. And they called up, offered me the job and that's when I got to Washington. And then I was on television here for 40 years.

Kevin: That's an awesome story.

Campbell: That's my story. That's going to do it. [Laughter] I think I just answered all seven of your questions.

[Laughter]

Kevin: Pretty much. But that's a great story. One of the things that I gathered from what you are saying is that it's interesting how life's journey, unbeknownst to you, pushes you and molds you into – like you said your father was a pianist. That's what you wanted to do. But then you're like, "No, that's not for me." And then coming up in photography class and I think from that, you can kind of gauge framing – how to tell a story with a photo – because that's all that a film is. It's a series of still images. Then coming into script writing. All these things make who you are.

And so going into the next question following up with that would be: how did you find your voice as a critic? Because your friend, Dick Dyszel, said you're "honest without being mean and vindictive" and that you're not a "mean-spirited" reviewer. But for those of us in the Washington area that watched you for many years, humor is a huge part of how you come to the film. And so, there's always this lightheartedness. I mean even just now in the interview, you're cracking jokes and everything. But I think for the future film critic, that was one thing that I had trouble with. Like, "Am I doing this right?" So, how did you find your voice as a film critic?

Campbell: Well, the first thing is that I was working in local television. So local television, especially back then, you had to appeal to a broad cross-section of people from every class and every walk of life. I was working in a broad medium. So I always stayed kind of broad – as far as the reviews go. I've stuck to this pretty much all my life. I rated a movie based on, "Did it fulfill its promise to get you to go see it in the first place? Did it do what it promised you? Was it entertaining?" That's another way of keeping it broad. And, "Is it worth the 15 bucks?" or whatever it cost to go to a movie now.

The other thing is – my first success was doing sort of stand-up comedy, emcee work and then radio work. And in television, my first success really was doing these kind of feature stories that were funny, the kind of stories that used to run at the end of the news. They don't run them anymore for various reasons, partly because it's hard to sustain doing that every day. I kind of grew up in a naturally funny family. So the humor was just kind of built into me but I also used it as a way of staying broad.

Consultants now – especially in television news – don't like movie reviews because a movie reviewer gets up there, slams something and if you – the viewer – like it, he or she might actually make you feel bad about yourself. So that was not part of the formula in those days.

And my approach especially because I was a reporter is that – okay, I mean I never studied film criticism. I took one film class where we made a movie but I didn't learn much from it. My approach always was that I wanted to be the average person and I wanted to talk in the same manner that you would talk if you were out on a date or on a night with your friends or wife after you've seen the movie.

So the short answer to your question is: I grew up with humor and I've always used humor and humor has helped me.

Kevin: That answers that. That makes a lot of sense and I think that's going to be super helpful for folks that are picking up this book.

Next question is: if it's true that there are only 7 basic

plots in the world, how do you keep a fresh eye for every movie that you see? Because we see so many every year, how are you able to just come with a fresh eye every time you see one of these films?

Campbell: Well, I mean you just have to keep an eye up for somebody who is able to do something new with those 7 plots. So for instance right now, Black Panther is really thrilling because they take the same old superhero. The superhero genre has really been done to death.

Kevin: [Laughter] Right.

Campbell: A good guy and a bad guy, the bad guy is threatening the world. And in the second act, the effects of the bad guy thing goes on. In the third act, the good guy fights the bad guy. The bad guy appears to be winning and then the good guy prevails.

Well, Black Panther went beyond that. They gave a back story that gave you the background of a hidden civilization and of the tension between this hidden civilization and our civilization, say in Oakland. And also the tension between families and between brothers and their sons and a generational passing down of values and feelings. Black Panther makes a really deep dive and also, its use of music and set design, character roles, men and women, is thrilling.

So Black Panther is a good example of a movie that can re-energize a genre that is the same old thing. I mean it all goes back to Shakespeare.

Kevin: In some ways, Arch, I'm just getting caught up and I'm thinking "Yeah, he is totally right." I totally enjoyed Black Panther for all the reasons that you stated and I think

Coogler is – he's just got a gift, like that was number three. For me, I gotta see three films that this director had done and just done well. And so, he just cemented himself in my top directors. But you're absolutely right.

Campbell: Yeah. And the other thing about Black Panther is the villain and the hero have shades. The hero is not totally good. He is more human. And the villain actually has got a point.

Kevin: [Chuckle] Right.

Campbell: So it's more like our life. So anyway, the answer is: you look for something that can take one of those plots and re-energize it. I was looking around the other day. Now, we're in this time which is having effect on movies and on critics. But we are in a time when you can access almost anything you want to watch because of streaming and the internet. What television can do now – I watched Alfred Hitchcock's The 39 Steps which he made in 1935. And that's the basis for almost every thriller made since because it's the wrong man pulled into a mystery, accused of doing something he didn't do, chasing after a criminal and being chased and a girl is involved. And then it's solved. And we go on. And that's 80 or 90 years old.

Kevin: So, what advice do you have for the up-and-coming critic?

Campbell: I think critics today need to be aware of the fact that movies are in a changing position. The position of film in our society is different now than it was 90 years ago. Ninety years ago, the movies were like our iPhones. They were this brilliant technology, unbelievable pictures moving on the screen. And they would develop with the use of new innovations. So we went from silent to sound to spectacle.

And then in the '60s – '60s and '70s and even '80s – the movies were where you went because they could do things in movies that they couldn't show on television. The movies were really the cutting edge medium. Well now, they're not. Now, the cutting edge is on cable. And now, the movies are more likely to disappoint than to thrill.

So, I would say anybody going into film criticism is going to have to recognize that. And anybody going in the film criticism is going to have to identify their audience. Who is your audience? Is it the person who goes to one movie a year which pretty much describes the movie-going audience? Is it the 16-year-old kid who goes to every superhero film because he wants to get out of the house and maybe meet a girl or a friend or whatever. So my advice is to identify your audience and identify the importance of what you're talking about.

Kevin: Kind of going off of that, you talked about in the beginning of the film, you had The Arrival of a Train at La Ciotat, the Lumière brothers. And it was rumored that at the time, people were running away from the screen because they had never seen something like that. They thought the train was going to hit them. And so you're right, we really evolved in film and the medium and technology in which it is made.

So, could you talk a little bit about adaptation? How does one adapt to change in time, technology and how we experience movies? Because with a career that spans over four decades, you've definitely been able to do that.

Campbell: Right now, I'm on a podcast. And the line is, "Where did the dinosaurs go to die?" [Laughter] I was very fortunate and I was fairly well-paid for most of my career. Right now, I'm working for pennies or for free. [Pause] So where am I going with this? [Laughter] Right now on my podcast, we talk about streaming and cable as much as we do movies because movies don't have the same position they used to have. And anybody going into film criticism is going to have to recognize this.

Right now, television news – which is where I really worked – has changed and morphed into something completely different than 40 years ago. Television news is about breaking news and weather. It's not about film criticism. There's one guy on TV, Kevin McCarthy, and he is on a morning show! So all I can say is that that world has changed. I think broadly, you need to – there's more to discuss than just films.

The Wire ushered in the 60-hour movie and that's what we're getting now on cable. I've seen several things this year that are just thrilling to watch. I watched Ozark. And the first season was 13 Hours. The Crown – the story of Queen Elizabeth, I think that was 15 hours in the second season so we're up to about 30 hours of that. And the shows on cable are designed to be binged. Binge-watching has changed everything.

So however you write, you need to know your audience. If your audience is a tiny sliver and they're only interested in independent films, then that's where you go. If your audience is broad, then you have to take a bigger look and look at the big picture. Right now, the big picture is that the most creative work is being done by cable.

Kevin: All right. So I got two more questions and then we're out. So the first question is: why is the film critic important? Or the flip-side would be: is a film critic not important?

Campbell: Well, there are two ways to answer that. [Laughter] I always consider myself a reviewer rather than a critic. So a reviewer is important because he or she gets the word out that, "Hey, Mindhunter is a great series on cable. You should check this out and see it." Or that, "Hey, Black Panther actually does something new and different and it's worth watching whether you're a superhero fan or not."

So as a reviewer, it's getting the word out and achieving a certain amount of credibility of, "Oh, that person knows what he or she is talking about. Yeah, I'll check that out."

As a critic which – and I never was really a critic – a critic helps you understand the movie after you've seen it. So, you don't need a critic to analyze the remake of Death Wish. [Laughter] But critics kind of help you see Black Panther a little differently or a little more clearly.

I saw a movie the other night, Thoroughbreds, which just thrilled me. It was really new and exciting. These two rich girls are bored and one of them is mad at her stepfather. They got nothing better to do so they start planning a murder. And it is highly erotic and very sexy and does not feature or include any nudity or any love scene. And yet, there is a tension and overlay with this thing that is just thrilling.

So I'm a reviewer. A critic, like Ann Hornaday, can help you understand why you like a movie. Why you like a movie includes plot, acting, set design, music, and the way the whole thing comes together.

Kevin: Arch that is an incredible answer. Wow! That actually [Chuckle] really just helped me in so many ways. I love how you put that together so concisely.

All right. The last question, I think you've already kind of hit this, but just to have consistency across the board: where do you see film criticism headed?

Campbell: I think like everything else, it's going to be headed toward a niche. I kind of regret that film reviewing and criticism are no longer as broad-based as it used to be. But the film world is no longer as broad-based as it used to be. And a lot of films now come out and they are reviewed. Do we really need a review of Death Wish? Do we really need a review of the live action Beauty and the Beast?

So I think it's headed where the audience is headed. And it seems to me that the audience for film is mostly niched with occasional movies like Black Panther or Star Wars or Beauty and the Beast that have huge reach beyond just being a movie.

CHAPTER 3

LESLIE COMBEMALE

Name: Leslie Combemale

Medium: Online

Outlet: patch.com, cinemasiren.com, The Credits

Years active: 15

Top 3 movies: Night of The Hunter, Cover Girl, Blade Runner

Favorite Director: Lynn Ramsey

Leslie Combemale has cultivated a unique array of experience and skill that enhances all the projects in which she becomes involved. She is an international expert in art, a respected film journalist, and a successful business owner of an art gallery open for over 25 years. As a professional film critic and industry insider, Leslie writes reviews and conducts interviews for numerous sites online, including the MPAA's The Credits and her own CinemaSiren.com. She also founded San Diego Comic Con's Women Rocking Hollywood panel, which celebrates the achievements of women in film, in collaboration with Women in Film: LA.

Leslie is one of those beautiful souls who warms up a room and rarely meets a stranger. There's no question about what and who she stands for: women and underrepresented voices! Her Women Rocking Hollywood panel at SDCC has grown year after year since its inception. Proving that a space for women to be heard and celebrated in the film industry is needed and wanted. We need more advocates for the voiceless and less visible people in Hollywood. Her work with women in the industry is appreciated and important! Leslie possesses a rare worldview and dedication to honesty and thorough research that her readers, audiences, and clients appreciate.

Kevin: When did you first fall in love with film?

Combemale: I used to watch cartoons with my dad when I was a little kid, and you know I grew up in Europe. I grew up in Italy and France. And so, I saw a lot of films on TV that were musicals and there were more films that were not played as much in – which I didn't find out until later – that were not the same as much as in the United States. And so, even as a little kid, like I'm talking like 4, 5, 6, 7 I saw lots of black and white films, lots of really old films. I fell in love with World War II propaganda films as a five or six old. And I love Louis Armstrong and Lena Horne and you know jazz musicians because I was really into jazz. And so, I liked to watch movies that had jazz musicians in them.

And so, I've loved the movies since I was a little kid. And I was fascinated with timing. Which is so geeky to say! But I was fascinated with timing, in terms of animation timing and comedic timing because I used to watch a lot of Chuck Jones cartoons. And he is famously a genius of timing. So that got me really interested, even as a little kid, in how music and film worked together and how the elements of filmmaking come together to coalesce into something cohesive or not. And, so I was already kind of – I've always – I loved loving movies. I don't like to rip them apart, because so many people make up a finished film. But even as a little kid, I was looking at what worked and what didn't work.

Kevin: OK. That's pretty awesome.

Combemale: Again, an answer, most people aren't going to be likely to say. [Laughter] So yeah.

Kevin: Oh, right, right. But that's what – that's the cool part about this. It's hearing where everyone kind of comes from. And, I'm sure that probably that kind also helped with the art gallery and everything, so the...

Combemale: Yes.

Kevin: ...the next question is what drew you to the art of film criticism? And, so specifically what drew you to talking about a film and what makes it. And I'm sure maybe even art gallery kind of fits into an answer as well.

Combemale: So, let's see, I always wrote, I studied poetry in college. I went to school for acting. I studied music. So, I mean I love the arts. I love a variety of arts. And I went to school at the same time as a bunch of other people who actually got famous. And saw their work and saw I wasn't nearly as good in terms in acting.

So, I was not as good as they were but I was fascinated by their craft and by the work they were doing. And as part of that, I also had to learn stage craft. And I studied the history of visual art and there were all of these elements. Because when I was in school, you know being European, the aesthetic, the way that people go to school is very different. We base all of our study in

– most of us – in more of an apprenticeship perspective, right?

So, I was always looking for these – for talented people who could teach me something. And there was a great writer, he was teaching at the school I wanted to go to so I studied with him. And I studied poetry with a really great poet. And I worked with this guy who was like a film historian. And so, I just had gotten all this information and I love to write but I don't like fiction. I mean I like to read fiction, but I don't like to write it. And then at the same time I've always been a feminist. Not a feminist in a way that it is like, "Please hold the door for me and then pay for my dinner and then…" you know, not that kind of feminist. The kind where – an equalist. And from that perspective I noticed early on, that there were not a lot of women with a voice.

And then around, when I opened my art gallery, first I went and worked for someone else who was opening of the first five animation galleries in the world. And I learned all about animation and became friends with all of these animators who since died. We're talking about Frank Thomas, Ollie Johnston, Marc Davis, Chuck Jones, Friz Freleng and Jay Ward. I mean just all of these amazing artists that have since passed away and I was fascinated by their stories and their artistry. And how much went into the works they did as filmmakers, as animators, and as story artist. And so, from the very beginning, when I was selling animation, I was really interested in the fact that when people came in the art gallery they didn't think that it was real art and that it was just for kids. But when people walked in to the store, they were thrown back into their childhood and their experiences and their memories. And a lot of times it related to people they've lost and family that meant a lot to them. And there was a lot of power on that.

So I got to understand pop culture as an international phenomenon that affected in a really powerful positive way, people's personal lives and their perspectives, and what was important to them. And as a result of that, I started writing. When computers became a thing more, I started writing blogs about it. At this point, a bunch of them had died. I had all this information that other people didn't have. And then I met John Alvin who created the art for more than 250 movie poster campaigns. He did the movie poster for Blade Runner, E.T., Young Frankenstein, Beauty and the Beast, The Lion King and all of that. At the same time I'm writing about these artists and what they've been, what influence they'd had and what importance they have in the history of film.

And it's just kind of – one of my friends worked for a newspaper and said, "You should write film reviews. You know, we're always talking about movies, and you have background in writing, you should write the reviews for the newspaper which was the Herndon Observer - since defunct." And so, I was like, "That sounds a good idea. OK." So, I started doing it and it happened really fast. A bunch of people started reading my stuff and I loved doing it. I always had a focus on the women in the films, noticing more and more that even if a movie was about a girl, she wasn't represented necessarily in the most three-dimensional way. And that got me more and more curious about the movies that were coming out, TV shows that were on, and how girls and women were represented both in front of and behind the camera.

Kevin: How did you find your voice as a critic? Because I think you're starting to get into that.

Combemale: Yeah. Well, I mean I needed the back story

because it's a weird way of getting into it. I wrote for a newspaper and then they went out of business. And I mean I owned an art gallery so I was focused on that. And it always for me, always, has been about promoting, spotlighting, and highlighting women and the work they are doing in film and diversity. It's also LGBTQ, and people of color. You know, I really just wanted to focus on that. And so my perspective, my interest was always to find platforms wherein I could choose what I wanted to write about.

And, I will write a review about a movie I want to really dissuade people from seeing. But on the whole, I really try to pick interviews and reviews of films that are not getting attention, that nobody – that are going to fall under the radar because nobody really needs another person to review, for example, Avengers you know, Infinity War. No one cares, because they're going to go anyway.

In fact I wrote a scathing review a couple of times. One time, a lot people listened and avoided it which was great because it was really misogynistic. And then another time I wrote about a Transformers movie, which one of them I really hated, and it broke a billion dollars very quickly. So, I realized it just didn't really matter when I wrote – and also, I was finding the outlets that would let me decide what I was going to review, and who I was going to interview. And that's how I've done it. I just curved out my own voice as a film critic, and you know, a promoter of women and film in places where they let me pick the movies and promote the films and write about the films that I think people to know about.

Kevin: Got it. So, if it's true that there are only seven basic plots in the world, how do you keep a fresh eye for

every movie that you see?

Combemale: Well, you know what, that's like saying there was already a band called The Who, so why is anyone a rock musician? You know there maybe only seven plots, well there are only twelve notes you know, in a scale. There's nothing new under the sun, right? I'm sure I'm not the first person to have said that in answering that question.

There are a million ways to tell a story and bring something fresh to it. It maybe that there are only a few plots, but where are the women in those plots? They're not represented in a three-dimensional and complicated way a lot of the time and certainly not in studio films. So, it's pretty easy to keep a fresh perspective because I'm looking at it from the perspective of a woman who wants to be seen as someone who can have a dissenting opinion, can be angry, can speak out, and still be lovable and still be interesting and still be sexy, or choose to not be sexy, whatever it is. So, it's very easy to keep a fresh perspective on that – coming from that place.

Kevin: What advice do you have for the up and coming critic and movie reviewer?

Combemale: I would say that there are plenty of places that are already reviewing all of the blockbusters and that what we need is champions of the underdogs. And that they need to learn how to write correctly and well. And, they need to learn about the history of film. I think that just because you have a computer and you know how to speak English, does not mean you know how to review a movie. I think it's really important.

And I would highly recommend women who love films to speak out and say what they think and how they feel about them.

Because we need more voices that are coming from a feminist place and that are championing films that are falling under the radar. With print and big media going out of business and losing money, a lot of them are not covering nearly as many films as they were. It's so important for films that are being made, that are complex and well constructed to be seen and for people to know about them. So, my recommendation is to take your perspective as an individual and tackle the films that are not being seen or heard about. That's what I would suggest.

Kevin: Awesome. Why is the film critic important? Or do you think the film critic isn't important?

Combemale: I think film journalism is important. I don't think we need two million think pieces on the same thing. What we need is thoughtful consideration, you know, considered and thoughtful writing and well-researched writing. We don't need clickbait. I think that it's important to champion good film. I think that's more important than being a critic. Because I think criticism is actually more complicated and more nuance than a lot of people who are picking up their computers and writing something that gets put on Rotten Tomatoes are aware of or care about. How about that for an answer? [Laughter] That's bitchy and appropriate.

Kevin: [Laughter] I love it, I love it. That was a good answer. All right, final question, where do you see film criticism headed?

Combemale: Well, I hope it's headed in a place where more diverse voices are speaking about more diverse film. And that connectivity, the ability to connect via the web and through new media, offers a bigger opportunity for women, people of color, LGBTQ, and trans people. All voices to be out there championing films that represent them. And I think that's where we're headed. I hope that's where we're headed, because I think people undervalue and underestimate the positive elements of social media. Because, for example, my Women Rocking Hollywood Panel at San Diego Comic-Con, I put on YouTube. Usually I get 75 to 100,000 people that watch it and they don't watch a minute, they watch 45 minutes. And these are women who are changing the face of film and television and staking a claim in an otherwise white male-dominated environment.

Kevin: Mm-hmm.

Combemale: And I think the future should be for everyone and about everyone. And that's our task; that's our challenge. The challenge of people who are younger and coming up is do they research, learn how to do it, become good at it and then be a champion. That's what the future should be. Will it be? I don't know. But we could all die tomorrow so it doesn't really matter. [Laughter] Trump could kill us all so, whatevs. So, go see a good movie, right?

[Laughter]

Kevin: Right.

CHAPTER 4

DOUGLAS DAVIDSON

Name: Douglas Davidson

Medium: Online, New Media

Outlet: Elements of Madness, Cine-men

Years active: 5

Top 3 movies: Superman: The Movie, Army of Darkness, Big Trouble In Little China

Favorite Director: Richard Donner

It's of little surprise that **Douglas Davidson** found himself drawn to studying film in both his undergrad and graduate school years after growing up in a household that loved watching movies. Though his professional vocations took him in a myriad of directions – even all the way to Johns Hopkins University to earn an M.A. in Communications – he's always found a way to work his love of cinema into his life. Created in 2012 as a means of keeping busy, Elements of Madness is now an online review vessel for Douglas to pour every ounce of geekdom into reviews of upcoming releases and a monthly Coming Soon series. His greatest pride as a writer is his June 2016 induction into the NC Film Critics Association, of which he is currently an active member. In October 2018, he was verified as a Rotten Tomatoes approved individual critic. In

April 2019, he was inducted into the Southeastern Film Critics Association. In September 2019, he was inducted into the Critics Choice Association.

In addition to running EoM, he is also a Senior Contributor Film Critic for Charlotte-based arts and culture blog CLTure, as well as a freelance critic for the newspaper Mountain Xpress, a contributing Film Critic for entertainment website Pretty Vacant One, a contributing Film Review Member for online film community FilmFed, and a co-host of The Cine-Men podcast on the Poprika Podcast Network.

Douglas is well accomplished, but he's extremely humble and A MACHINE! I'm talking a pure T-1000 when it comes to churning out film reviews. With nearly a daily review or film blog of some sort on his site, it's hard to imagine how he balances it all, but he does!

Kevin: When did you first fall in love with film?

Davidson: I wish I could pinpoint a year on it, but it was when I was a kid. My mom's side of the family, they still do this trip in Destin, Florida where it's just sort of a reunion. Everybody that can come down for about a week hangs out by the beach. I have two older brothers and a mess of cousins. Just a mess of cousins, and all of them have now had kids so it's just more and more and more.

But when we were little we would get together at night and watch movies. I remember watching Back to the Future and Back to the Future II when we were all together. We had a hospitality suite because we had all these hotel rooms. Everybody baked food and kept stuff in there so we could do a communal meal and stuff like that.

I remember watching Willy Wonka & the Chocolate Factory in there, and just being this little kid, 5, maybe 6 years old. Watching all these stories and hanging out with my family and watching these movies was just – it was the highlight for me of that trip. Our parents got us all airbrush t-shirts so that we knew that we were all related and stuff like that.

Kevin: Woah!

Davidson: Oh yeah, oh yeah, we went all out. I mean I haven't been on that trip in decades now, but it's still something that I can look back on. It's one of my first memories of this [movies] being something I love. It's something I can share. My family loved going to the movies. My thing to do on my birthday in December was go to a movie. Being Jewish, it's Christmas, where do you go? The movie theater. So I mean all these big things have always been associated with cinema and for me, it's just about the stories. I love a good story.

So growing up, realizing that this is something that a group of people can sit around, experience together but even experience differently because we may pick up something different. We may see it from a different perspective. Our experiences may pull something out that may not for someone else and just talking about it. So for me, it was just a little kid being down in Destin, Florida.

Kevin: Awesome. So what drew you to the art of film criticism? Because I think it's one thing to just watch a movie, but what drew you to the art of film criticism?

Davidson: I think it was the fact that my mom is an academic. She is retired now but she was a history professor both in college and in high school and she has taught English in any number of things. My dad, while he is not an academic in the professional world, he also has an analytical mind. I remember my dad – I was so excited for Aladdin. I took my dad like, "We've got to go and go see this," as a little kid. And I remember my dad looking at me and going, "So what was the moral of that?" And I looked at him and went, "It was an animated movie, dude. Can't you just enjoy that?"

It was that aspect of my parents wanting us to look deeper. You can take in a story and go, "That was fun. This was a fun ride." But at the same time, what is it that's going on with it? What is it they're trying to convey and why are they doing it?

Originally, I was an English major before I switched to communications in undergrad and studied cinema. It was the fact that an author's words can be interpreted however you want. Sometimes the author says, "Yes! This is exactly what I meant." Other times, it's really for the reason undetermined. With cinema, I found that there's so much more than words. It's this meeting of music and visual imagery and language that even language changes in its meaning from tone and delivery, all of this stuff, it just became fascinating about the different interpretation.

So for me, it's just the way that we all look at it; we can all look at the same thing and it comes across differently. Growing up in sort of an academic household, I just sort of took that and applied it to that and I love it. It's fascinating to me how everyone can watch something and go, "This is great. This is terrible." But let's discuss why, because it's not enough to just say "thumbs up, thumbs down." That's easy. Anybody can do that. With criticism and review, it's about actually discussing it. What is it about that thing that was good? What is it about that thing that was bad? What is the effectiveness here that we're talking about? So that's sort of the long-winded answer but I think that's sort of what drew me into it. Just an academic background.

Kevin: No. I think that's a great answer. And piggybacking off of that, like you said, anybody can be a critic these days and I think a lot of times, because there are so many voices that are out on a particular movie, sometimes it's hard to stick to your gut and to your guns. So for somebody that's like coming up, how did you find your voice as a critic?

Davidson: Well, I began by drawing on what comes naturally to me, and that is an academic evaluation. I have a Masters in Communication and so just looking at things from a standpoint of what is it that it's trying to accomplish and how well does it do that? It always drives me crazy–you talked about film criticism today, and how there are so many more voices. There are also more people going, "Not everything could be the Godfather." Well, here's the thing. When you're watching Deadpool 2, no one is expecting that to be the Godfather. They're just measuring it against the best Deadpool 2 it can be and does it accomplish that goal. So for me trying to find my voice and yeah, there are so many voices and so many critics that I grew up watching, critics that are contemporaries that I read that I love for their view, but I had to figure out what is my voice? And my voice is from an academic perspective so I think about it in terms of effectiveness. I think about it in terms of what is this director was trying to accomplish and how well did they do that?

Anytime I try to stray from that, even if it's silly or it's fun, for me, it doesn't feel like me. And so, I always – it's trial and error. A lot of it error because you can imitate other people but that's not you. So for me doing it, I had to look at it from an academic way. The more I tweak it, the more that I write, the clearer my voice becomes. Even then it's still changing but my approach – it's just tweaking the approach rather than the voice itself, if that makes any sense whatsoever.

Kevin: Yeah, I totally get it. I think it makes a lot of sense and that's great advice. The next question is, if it's true that there are only 7 basic plot points or plots in the world, how do you keep a fresh eye for every movie that you see?

Davidson: Well, the way that I look at it is really simple and it's sort of what I said before. What is the story that this film is going to try and convey? With the film that I'm reviewing right now, it would be very easy to go, "Well, this other film did this and this other film did that and why couldn't it be those films?" Well, it's not those films. It's this film.

So even if there are 7 different plots, there are different ways to tell that story. I think of it in the same way that as a teacher. I meet, let's say 75 students a semester. Each one of them are unique but each one of them are similar. They might come from the same city. They might come from the same religious background, and the same economic status. Who knows? But the way that they look at the world is going to be different. It's the same way with cinema. If we look at Sean Baker, he is going to have a different viewpoint of the world than James Gunn, than Steven Spielberg, than Richard Donner.

Pick a director, man, woman, any age, and it doesn't matter the story that they're trying to tell. They're telling it through their lens, and their experience. So as far as how do you try and keep it fresh? You try and think of it as – it's not about is this is a story I've seen, but who is this person and what story are they trying to tell?

Kevin: Awesome. All right. So what advice do you have for the up and coming critic?

Davidson: The up and coming critic? Patience. Patience. Don't try and be first. It's not about being snide. It's not about – criticism isn't about breaking things apart. It's not about saying, "This sucks." It's not about being mean. It's not about being personal.

Criticism in its truest form is about being able to articulate for people what works or doesn't work and why. It's about being able to identify it and discuss it. It's very easy today with – our culture is driven by likes, retweets, shares, et cetera. It's the metric system we use for eyeball. So I've got click bait everywhere. It's really easy for new critics to go, "Well, I need to be dynamic. I need to be abrasive. I need to create content that rips these movies apart." That's not what film criticism is though. It's not what it's supposed to be.

It's not enough to be sarcastic and funny. It actually has to say something. True film criticism should be an analysis of what the film is and what it's trying to do and how it did it. And it's not enough to go, "Oh well, the Godfather is amazing film and we need to keep it up on its pedestal." Yeah, but if it doesn't work, we need to explain why. And if you go to say, the other end of the spectrum with Deadpool 2, well, it's perfect. It's a great movie. It is a perfect sequel for what it's trying to accomplish. And for the world in which Deadpool lives, it accomplishes that in a great way. Could you be sarcastic about it? Absolutely. Could you do the same thing with the Godfather?

Sure. But that doesn't make it interesting, articulate, or informative.

So the best advice I could give to an up and coming film critic is be true to yourself but also be true to the work. If you want to be a critic, you actually have to do that. Be critical. Analyze. Look at the work and discuss the work. Don't try and be clever.

Kevin: That's great advice. All right. So why is the film critic important? And by that I mean like I guess the flip-side is even, are we important? I think for those of us that are true critics, we understand what we bring to films. But I do think that in some ways corporate culture has taken what we talk about and made it into this "how can I get more likes?", like you just talked about.

So to go back to the question, why is the film critic important?

Davidson: Well, I think the film critic is important for, really two reasons, one is because film is art. It is. It's again, I'll just keep this comparison, Deadpool 2 versus the Godfather. Each one, no matter what you think of them, no matter how you turn up your nose at one or the other, they're both art. So a discussion of them will take place. And as we live in this consumable society, we're one step away from They Live really, that we are trying to consume as much as possible but that doesn't mean that we're digesting it.

Film critics help people to digest. They provide an opportunity either before a film to get an idea of it, or after a film to think about things that they may have seen or maybe things that they didn't. We help to be able to pick things up that they may not have noticed. And that's where I think film criticism is important in terms of the art of it.

And you wouldn't have, by the way, any of these metrics, the Rotten Tomato and what have you, without critics because it's not just users, it's also the critics themselves. But the other reason why I think film criticism is important or particularly the film critic is that people that get into this business, for the most part, I can't say everybody, I don't know everybody, but the people that I've spoken to that I've engaged with locally and internationally, the people that I read, they are not in this business because they want to tear film apart or they want to make it smaller. Instead, they want to make it larger. They love film. They love storytelling.

So they want to see film as you and I have discussed. You want to see as much as possible. You may not be able to see everything, but you want to see as much as you can and talk about it. A film like The Florida Project from last year was a very small film but due to screenings and some festivals where critics were, it got more and more attention. Did it get enough attention? No, I don't think so, but it did.

There are a lot of small films that come out every year, many films that don't even get noticed but thanks to film critics writing, talking, and being engaged in that world, they are able to get the word out for films. Now, we're not a part of the promotional aspect of things, but just like anything else – we love stories and we want people to know about them. So that's sort of the – that's the two reasons why I think film criticism is important, film critics in particular.

Kevin: Sweet. So where do you see film criticism headed?

Davidson: Well, the realist in me that has studied digital technology, is concerned that film criticism is headed to a point where critics themselves are going to be utterly devalued. Because you've got instantaneous social commentary, everyone is going to be so interested in what the surface level discussion is going to be that the idea of deep, thoughtful discussion is going to go away. That's looking at it from a technological perspective and how we use technology.

However, I also think, particularly as my generation gets older and new generations are coming up, you're seeing a larger trend towards physical content, moving away from digital uses. So CD sales maybe dwindling but vinyl is going up. There's sort of this push towards the analog, which theoretically would mean that these are people that are looking for something they can put their hands on and film criticism is something where they can do that with books, magazines, newspapers. Sure they're not making the money that they used to but that's where film critics live. Even if they live online, they're still publishing. They're still reading.

So the pessimistic part of me feels like we're getting to a point where we're not – where film criticism isn't going to be as relevant. But on the other hand, I see real hope. And particularly being in the classroom, there are some really bright and articulate kids that are coming up and that are not just looking at things at face value. They want to examine. They want to be critical in sense of understanding. So, I feel hopeful. I feel hopeful that there's going to be a bigger push the further we get to just thoughtfulness and engagement.

CHAPTER 5

ADELLE DROVER

Name: Adelle Drover

Medium: Online

Outlet: Roll Credits

Years active: 6

Top 3 movies: Lord of The Rings, Pan's Labyrinth, Spirited Away

Favorite Director: Wes Anderson

Adelle Drover is a film journalist, video producer and serious coffee fanatic. She's usually found writing film notes in a cozy London coffee shop. I came across Adelle's Roll Credits YouTube channel after seeing Chris Stuckmann's Stuckmann Suggests video, in which he recommended up and coming new voices of movie review YouTubers. After checking out her work, it was evident that Adelle was passionate about film.

Honestly, I was glad I followed her work because most of the time in the business, you hear weekly reviews from men. I'm a huge fan of diversity and for me, it was great to hear a woman's take on the latest films that are out. Adelle's reviews are always lighthearted, eloquent, and thorough, but they feel like you are talking to a good friend. So many people who start YouTube channels like to create a persona that emulates other popular YouTubers. Adelle's aptitude to be herself is a part of what makes her YouTube channel stand out, as her originality is worth watching, but more importantly in the space, merits coming back for!

Kevin: All right, Adelle. So when did you first fall in love with film?

Drover: Right. Well, I feel like I had always loved film growing up as a child. But the first time that I really noticed film in a really profound way was the age of 12 and walking into the cinema with my family to watch The Lord of the Rings: The Fellowship of the Ring. And that was a movie I knew nothing about, and thought nothing of it. My dad was a fan of the books when he was a kid.

And when I walked into that movie and saw the world building that they had created, I was just absolutely transported in I think a way that I had probably never experienced before in this whole fantasy world. And when I walked out of that movie, not only did I love the story, but I wanted to know how the filmmakers had done that. And so, I started doing all that research, behind the scenes, the director's commentary, everything. I just needed to know everything! So that's where it all really sort of started for me.

Kevin: I think it's kind of interesting because one of the things that at least on your site, it says "we love movie magic". And so what you just kind of described was the magic of cinema and how it can transport you. So before we get into the next question, maybe you could talk a little bit about what movie magic is to you?

Drover: For me, movie magic is definitely those moments in cinema where your eyes open wide and you just cannot believe what you are seeing, and what you are experiencing. It's so immersive. And for me, I find cinema a medium that is a lot more immersive than reading a book or going to the theater. And that's different for everyone. But for me, that's just really, really apparent.

And when I'm watching a movie, I can be absolutely transported. I can love and appreciate a movie but even though that movie might not be in my preferred genre or it might not be a story that speaks to me personally, I can still love and appreciate the craft, the craftsmanship, and the visuals that have gone into creating the movie. Even if that movie is about a topic that isn't sort of my topic or a genre that isn't my kind of genre. I think I can appreciate the magic of just cinema in general.

Kevin: Got it. So what drew you to the art of film criticism and film reviewing? Because I feel like you do both.

Drover: Yeah. Yeah. And I feel like there is kind of – so for me, I am straddling that fence between what is movie reviewing and what is film criticism? And I've sort of developed the theory that the movie reviewing is more opinion-structured and just commentary-based about – from a personal experience bringing that to the film whereas film criticism leans on the more journalistic side of things. It's more analytical, maybe more structured, and formal in its dissection of the film.

So I feel like I have been sort of trying to sort of separate those – what's a film review versus what a film critic kind of is. Yeah, what do you think about that? I don't know. I'm still working on it.

Kevin: No. It's interesting because Arch Campbell, I think he put it perfectly. He said that a reviewer gets the

word out about a film whereas a critic helps you understand the movie after you've seen it. So the reviewer just kind of talks about it and talks about whatever, "Get Out was so awesome, blah, blah, blah." But then the critic actually helps you to understand what you watched. "Well, the cotton that he used to free himself is symbolic of cotton that slaves picked..." so you go more into that.

Drover: Right. Right. You drill down into more meaning and that kind of thing. Yeah. Yeah. I can definitely agree with that, which is also probably why in the beginning, I would never have associated myself with the word, "film critic" and I did always call myself a movie reviewer. That's sort of how I introduced myself and what I put in my bio online that I'm a movie fan, cine lover and movie reviewer. That's sort of how I classified myself.

And it really was for me. It was a really gradual evolution from being somebody who just wanted to share some opinions online about what I just saw at the movies yesterday to really wanting to go in more and dissect it more. I do have a background in film. I studied film analysis and history at university, and then went to film school.

So I sort of had that background playing in the back of my knowledge-base but at the beginning when I first came online and started reviewing movies on YouTube and the web, we definitely started as just opinion-based and just talking to friends online that approached to becoming a little bit more analytical I suppose.

Kevin: This is great. So the next question is, how did you find your voice as a critic? Because I feel as though when I first started, one, it's kind of hard to find a mentor and somebody to help you. Then two, because of that, I

eventually had to realize I shouldn't try to be like anyone else. Just be yourself. And so I think especially as a YouTuber, it can be easy to look other people because visually, you can just watch different videos and try to emulate something else that you see. But how did you find your voice?

Drover: Yeah, that's a really tough question. I think it's a really tough question for anyone. How does anyone find their voice and then sort of pull that out and bring that approach to what they're doing when they're approaching and analyzing movies?

I am first and foremost, I suppose I'm a YouTube movie critic so I am online. So finding my authentic voice and just being honest and true with what I was saying and if I didn't like a movie, just being upfront about that and not worrying what kind of feedback I was going to get from people who did love the movie.

I mean the online space can be really scary because I think the community can be anonymous for the most part and you can get hated out there. Everyone knows that trolls and haters are online. I've definitely had a fair share of that online too. But it kind of makes you stronger as well. It gives you more conviction in your opinions.

And from there, I think finding your voice as a critic isn't just something you do overnight. It's definitely something you develop, and you start by having mentors and looking up to what other people are doing. Remembering, maybe why you sort of got involved in it in the first place.

And then from there, from just emulating what your favorite

reviewers and critics are doing and their style of things, you can over time really develop your strengths and pull out your authentic voice.

Kevin: If you can, so we talk about like old school versus new school and like old school, you write up something in print and unless somebody wanted to write a letter to the paper, you're not going to get that instant feedback. And even like on TV, it's not that instant feedback versus today like you can literally post a tweet and then boom like it's an automatic response. People might be on your side or not.

But can you talk a little bit about what you were saying with dealing with trolls – because I think sometimes it can in some ways either cause us to dim our light a little bit or shrink back or you want to move with the crowd. But I think that what you are saying in terms of like being stronger because of it is really big and important. But at the same time, we do live in a world where we worry, "Am I going to get likes or will this get a thumbs-up or a thumbs-down?"

How do you manage that?

Drover: How do you manage putting yourself out there online to the world, to the sort of faceless internet in a way?

Kevin: (Laughs)

Drover: It's scary. It is definitely scary. And honestly, it's a big step. At first, I was not comfortable sharing my real name at all, which is why I created this pseudonym of Roll Credits, which is the name that I now go under with my channel and my website and all the reviews that I do because at first I was too scared to put my name to it in case I did have a wave of hate or even worse than a wave of just trolling. What cuts you even worse is when people disagree with your opinions and they have very valid arguments. And that's kind of even more challenging because what they are saying is absolutely valid in every single way and it's completely opposite to how you saw the exact same film, and that can be very daunting.

But it's also good. It pushes you to find that strongest stance and grow that conviction and your opinions. And over time, I think, learn to understand that it's definitely OK to disagree with your audience. And I've had people who have commented on my content and have absolutely disagreed with everything that I've said and then they've picked apart in great detail the reasons why I am wrong. It takes a while to learn to be able to go back to that person and say, "I appreciate what you're saying. I disagree", but maybe come back with some opposing points and you grow that discussion.

And I've had people that I might consider haters on my side who have grown into fans because I've had that ongoing discourse. And I think that's something that old school media and film critics don't get to have. I think that's a real positive of new media is that you can have a direct discourse with your readers, with your audience. And that's really exciting.

Kevin: I love that answer and I think that's so true because if you're able to kind of master your fears on that, I do think that like you said, you build. You even build your personal base in terms of how you understand movies, because everything is subjective, but then sometimes like you said, somebody might come with a point that's very valid. So that makes a lot of sense.

Next question is, if it's true that there are only 7 basic plots in the world, how do you keep a fresh eye for every

movie you see or TV show that you review?

Drover: This is a great question. You're right. I watch a lot of movies. I watch so many movies – I watch TV series as well. I probably do stick to the movie side of things but there have been many series that I have binged days' worth of episodes on. And I've watched a lot of stuff and I continue to watch a lot of stuff. I have to keep a movie diary just to keep track of everything that I'm watching because otherwise some of it, especially the things that are a little bit more generic and feel very familiar, those stories go in one ear and out the other. So I can sometimes forget that I've even seen a particular movie.

But yeah, how do you keep that fresh eye? Look, I don't know if I'm keeping the fresh eye for content. I think that film makers are constantly pushing the boundaries and they are the ones bringing the fresh stories and the fresh way to telling those stories. You can now film an entire movie on your smartphone. Do you know what I mean? They are really constantly pushing those boundaries to make it fresh for their audiences.

Kevin: Right.

Drover: And those are the movies that really stick out to me and I appreciate the filmmakers' intent to create something as fresh and as interesting and new as possible. But it's yeah, it's not easy.

Kevin: So I'm a little interested in that you said you keep a movie diary. Is it like an actual diary but about what you watched? How does that work?

Drover: I used to keep a – well, I originally started years ago. I had an obsession with saving all my printed ticket stubs and sticking them into a little book. That's years ago now, but that was how I had started just so I could flick back throughout the year and see how many movies I had seen and everything like that.

But you might know that those ticket stub printouts quickly fade over time. So if you went back through those books now, half the inks are gone. You can't see anything. So that's when I developed it into actually writing little notes in a little pocket-size journal that I'd just keep in my handbag wherever I went.

And now, I think in the past year, I've changed my method again and I use an online platform. I use the website called Letterboxd. They have a great – the catalog in there is unbelievable. I've got every single movie in there. And they have a really brilliant little function called Diary function where you can log the movie you've seen, the date you've seen it, and I always do that. And I can just scroll back throughout the months and see everything I've seen. Also, see the star rating. I can give a little rating out of 5 stars and it has made my life so much easier.

Kevin: That's awesome. I've seen Letterboxd and I've seen a lot of people use it but I have not gotten into it yet. So now that you've said it, I'm going to have to actually get into it because it is one of those things where I used to try to use Pinterest to kind of keep up with all the movies that I saw and just be like a running tab of what I saw. But even that is – it's so tedious to keep up with getting everything out there that you've seen. It's ridiculous. So all right, Letterboxd.

[Laughter]

Drover: Yeah, it's good. But like any other platform, it's just another account to manage so I don't use it to – you can review on there and write written reviews and everything. I don't use it for any of that. I purely use it for that diary function to catalog what I've seen. But yeah, it's a really great site actually. Yeah. I should use it more.

Kevin: OK. So before we get down to like the next question, I think because of what you've just said in regard to time management, and I think that because you, especially with YouTube, consistently put out new reviews or new videos, how do you manage your time to do that as well as red carpet events and screenings and things like that?

Drover: I ask myself that all the time. I think my friends and family ask me all the time too, how do I do it all? I mean the short answer is you just have to love it. You have to live and breathe it and make the time for it. But really, as far as my video creation- like you see the movie then you're going to write the film notes as any critic does. Then I've got to put some make-up on, get dressed up nicely then I've got to film and record my review then I've got to upload that – download that footage on to my computer and then I've got to sit there.

The edit process usually takes – I can do it pretty fast now, but by the time I cut out all my best points and put that into a video, overlay that with trailer footage, put on my watermarks and graphics, that's at least two hours. And to export it and upload that video file to YouTube is another hour. So it's a lot of work.

So it is hard to find time. I think I've gotten quite fast at it now. It has been four years since I've been producing content on YouTube now. Getting faster at it but yeah, it still does take a lot of time.

Kevin: Alright. So what advice do you have for the up-and-coming critic?

Drover: Advice for up-and-coming critics, this is tough. It's simple in a way but it's really hard to hear if you are somebody who is up-and-coming. And that is to find your authentic voice. It's something that we talked about earlier. And I think that in the online space, it's very crowded and it's very saturated. There are a lot of people who are creating online accounts and online profiles. Anyone in their bedroom can just be an "online critic."

So to really break through that white noise and find an audience, a loyal audience that are interested in what you have to say and your perspective on the movies that you are watching is not simple. It's not easy. And I think authenticity and building trust with your audience is just so key because I think new media is very different from that old style way of doing things where you have authority because you have done the education and you've gotten the job and that's your job title.

In the newspaper space, you write your article. You've got a title there, film critic, and that's the authority that you have for people to listen to you. Whereas nowadays when anyone can be a "film critic" online in their bedroom, it's a lot more difficult to carve out that trust with an audience and why will somebody click on your video and watch you and trust what you have to say without that sort of proof. So yeah, I think authenticity and finding your voice is really key.

Kevin: Sweet. So one of the things that a lot of people talk about lately especially with Rotten Tomatoes and all these different measuring systems is, is the film critic or movie reviewer important? Why is the film critic important or is the film critic not important in your opinion?

[Laughter]

Drover: I'm not going to choose that option. No, the film critic is important. It's vital. It's every part of – it's very much a part of the film. As the film itself, the writing and the directing and the production and the marketing, the film critic is sort of that head of the audience. It's that link between the film and the film's audience and theater goers. So the film critic or movie reviewer or however you want to sort of label it is just that direct connection.

The critic or movie reviewer is absolutely crucial and just as important as the production, the pre-production, production, and post-production on the movie itself because the critic is that direct line of trust between the movie and the audience. So, I think that the critic is the vital link between – in connecting the right audience to the movie.

So that's why I think a lot of movies, smaller Indie movies have found huge success through positive word of mouth and through movie reviewers spreading positive reviews and positive feedback and really encouraging people to pay the price of admission and take a chance on a movie that might not have had a huge marketing campaign. The movie might not be prominent on billboards and that kind of thing but they have done really well because people have spread the word and film critics have really elevated the message on the movie's behalf. So it's basically free advertising for the movie.

Kevin: Awesome. All right. So the last question is, where do you see film criticism and movie reviewing headed?

Drover: Now, you sent me the questions ahead of time. And this was the one question that I couldn't find an answer to because with how technology is going, I just – I just don't know where it's heading. I'm not sure how it's going to continue to evolve. It has already changed so much in the last 20 years. I think that as we move forward, we're going to start to see more and more voices join the space. Maybe we already have over the past few years.

But I think more and more people will feel confident to yeah, join the film critic's space because they have the resources, the resources, it's all available now like you don't necessarily have to have gone to a film school. You can be just a genuine fan and have just done your homework and watched a million movies under the sun and develop your strong opinions and your authentic voice that way.

So – but in terms of where it's heading, I don't know if I have a good answer for that. Sorry.

Kevin: No, it's OK. You don't have to have the answer.

Drover: I don't know what we will see next. I'm just mulling it over and just trying to come up with a genuine idea of how I feel about it. But I do think that as we continue with the digital revolution that we will see more and more people feel the confidence to join the space, and that will only be a good thing. I think maybe a lot of old school film critics might be intimidated or apprehensive about anybody being able to like I said before sit in their bedroom and just join the conversation and classify themselves as a film critic.

But I don't think that's something to be worried about because people who are genuine and people who genuinely have the passion and the love and are worth watching and listening to, they will definitely stand out from the crowd and they will go on and I think we will all be lucky to listen to what they have to say.

Kevin: Most def. All right. So one last question, I'm kind of fascinated, what is your setup for doing your YouTube reviews? So obviously, you got to have a good camera. At least for me looking at your videos, you have a camera, a key light, and you use a mic. So, do you want to talk a little bit about like what your setup is and how you- like you said, four years in, you kind of gotten it down to a machine.

[Laughter]

Drover: Yeah.

Kevin: So just talk a little bit about that.

Drover: Yeah. Well, I might have a different start to any budding critics wanting to get started on YouTube. And I might have had an advantage because I was a videographer before starting my channel. So I do have a lot of confidence with filming, with using a camera, with using lighting and editing and all that kind of stuff.

The camera that I started, my very, very first YouTube review video, four years ago, I was using a Canon DSL camera and I still use that exact same camera today. So while I've added lighting since I first started, I've grown my lighting kit along the way. I've got two soft box lights that I use. And yes, a microphone, a blue tooth microphone that I plug into my computer.

While I have grown those additional bits and pieces, I still use my exact same camera. I've seen people who do great reviews and they just use their iPhone. I have actually uploaded plenty of videos on my channel that have been filmed with my iPhone like blogs and Q&As and I've just used my iPhone for those because it's been convenient or because I've been out of my studio. And so I think that really does show that you can do it from any different level, from basic to intermediate to advance in terms of equipment. You can still get your voice out there.

CHAPTER 6

EPIC FILM GUYS

Name: Epic Film Guys

Medium: Online, New Media

Outlet: Epic Film Guys Podcast

Years active: 6

Nick's Top 3 movies: About Schmidt, American Beauty, The Fountain

Nick's Favorite Director: Alexander Payne

Justin's Top 3 movies: Batman (1989), John Carpenter's Halloween, The Terminator

Justin's Favorite Director: John Carpenter

The **Epic Film Guys** came to being in the Spring of 2014 after months of planning and discussion between Nicholas Haskins and Justin Esquivel. They were two guys who were extremely passionate about films, so much so that that everyone around them suggested they should record that passion for the world. Both Nick and Justin would agree that they were fast friends, but it was their bond over one specific film- Batman (1989)– that made them best friends. At the midnight release of Man of Steel in June 2013, they had their first taste of what their future would become when they were among many guests on the Extremely Loud and Incredibly Nerdy podcast.

Amazing Spider-Man 2 served as the launch point for the Epic Film Guys at the premiere showing at the Dickson City Regal IMAX. At that point in time, they were primarily just a video show, recording their reviews and random video segments and uploading them onto their YouTube page. By the end of 2014, their Facebook page had grown to well over one thousand followers, and the Epic Film Guys even started moving into scripted videos. Near the end of 2014, after Justin's wife got a lucrative job offer near Washington D.C., and as a result, the Epic Film Guys were separated. While it brought an end to the video reviews they did together (aside from the occasional special event), it also led to what is now their primary focus, the Epic Film Guys Podcast.

When I first met Justin, Picture Lock was a TV show recording out of Arlington Independent Media. He reached out to me via email about coming on the show and it was all love from that first meeting. These guys truly appreciate and admire film, and they love discussing it…as well as occasionally fighting over it. If you haven't listened to their podcast, you're missing out on a well-polished, tightly executed, completely unique, and oftentimes hilarious show that cares about film. It's their undeniable passion that oozes out of every show, Facebook showdown post, or IG story that creates a cinema loving culture that anyone would want to be part of!

Kevin: All right. So guys, let's start now. First question is, when did you first fall in love with film? And I guess we have Nick, if you go first.

Haskins: All right. Well, I mean Justin already knows the answer to this question. So it's Batman '89, baby. I was obsessed with that film. I'm still obsessed with that film really. I held an old boom box, when that movie first came out, up to the TV and recorded audio from the movie and listened to it on a Walkman. I've just been fascinated with film and the power of film to move you like emotionally, physically, and mentally. I absolutely love it. That's what taught me how to love film.

Esquivel: I hate to be lockstep with Nic. That's kind of the thing that drew us together into the world of movies. But when I was 5 years old, at the local drive-in theater, I remember like it was yesterday, it was the Airport Theater, Drive-In Theater in Johnson City, New York, June 23, 1989, opening night for Tim Bearn's Batman. I begged my parents for weeks seeing the ad, that giant bat symbol in the paper and I just could not wait to see it. And that was my first experience with a big budget blockbuster and I fell in love with movies after that.

Kevin: Man, that's kind of crazy. So to divert really quickly from the question but you guys share that love [of Batman]. How did you guys come together as the Epic Film Guys?

Haskins: Me? Was it debt collecting? I think it was debt collecting. Yes, it was at first. And then we worked at a debt collection place together and then we worked at an insurance place together. We were aware of each other before then. I dated a girl that worked at the newspaper when Justin worked at the newspaper. So we were at least aware of each other for a long time. And then the more he and I got to know each other, as we sat and talked, the more we just found this connection; this film connection.

And before long, we were working at 21st Century and Justin couldn't drive anymore for reasons, so I had to go pick him up every day for work. We would drive to and from work every day listening to film's scores and stuff. We sat right next to each other when we worked at that gig, we like – we practically lived together almost for quite a while there. And we lived and breathed movies every day all the time.

Kevin: Man, that's crazy. So where are you guys from again? It's something New York. What is it?

Haskins: Binghamton.

Esquivel: We say it Binghamton, yeah, Everyone calls is Binghamton. It's Binghamton. But I mean that's where we were both pretty much – it's the name of that larger area. There are smaller towns in there but we just said Binghamton for short. So yeah, Binghamton.

Kevin: All right. Sweet. So what drew you to the art of film criticism? And I know for you guys maybe you might consider yourself more of a movie reviewer. But what drew you to the art of breaking down movies and talking about it?

Esquivel: I think for me, it was just my love of film and movies in general. I found myself constantly thinking about it or discussing it. And it goes back to what Nick and I were just referring to in working together, we would – in between our work, we would constantly talk about movies and we would get into debates and we would just discuss it openly. And people would listen to us and a lot of other colleagues around us.

And it got to the point where- I forget who it was that said it. It might even have been Michael Vasquez, who is a gentleman who now has his own politics broadcast, who said, "Why don't you guys do something with this? Why don't you like actually just set up a camera or like record this and release it because you guys go back and forth. It's entertaining. You guys have a banter."

So I just took that as, "Hey, why don't we do that and we would turn our passion into something more?"

Haskins: Yeah. And for me, I studied film in college and I initially did a film studies minor when I was in college. And then film was always something that fascinated me way before I ever went to college so that's why I picked up the minor. And then there's just something about watching a film analytically that just stuck with me. I love to deconstruct things. Mentally I love to deconstruct them nuance-wise. I think beneath the surface of a film, that's where all good criticism lies.

I think I just love challenging myself to see things inside of a film. It's more than just the presentation of it. That's how I see them. I see – when I watch a film, I see the nuts and bolts of it up on screen. I don't just see the flash. I don't just see the fun, brainless, popcorn-y-ness of it and will get down sometimes because I don't just have fun at the movies. I get too nuts and boltsy but that's just me. I just love seeing films that way.

Kevin: So that kind of leads into the next question. And I think this is a really cool question for you guys since you're a duo. So individually but then also as the Epic Film Guys, how did you find your voice as a critic?

Haskins: I think for me, I'm a very larger than life kind of character and very boisterous. When I'm in a room, you know it. And I carry that over into my criticism. So I sprinkle a good bit of rhetoric and some hyperbole into everything I talk about. I always give honest ratings. I always say that the truth lies in my rating of the film.

But like if I find something that has even a little bit of a fault

– like when we reviewed A Quiet Place, a film I still rated an 8 out of 10, I hated one aspect of the film. So I went after it with a plow and I really, really dug into it. Justin and I get back and forth on stuff like that every once in a while, but I like my criticism to be as large – as bombastic I would say, as I am.

Esquivel: And for me as far as finding my voice, I mean it really came down to Nic and I coming together and really figuring out our chemistry together. I came from a background of playing live music. I was a vocalist in a bunch of metal and hard core bands since I was 14 years old. And when I started doing the film criticism movie review stuff with Nic, I was already done with that part of my life but I knew how to publicly speak and how to get on stage in front of people and kind of project myself as a personality.

So I kind of took that experience and put that into what I wanted to be as my persona because obviously, it's all fun to just sit down and write a review. But I want to be a personality like Nic and match that. And I think I found my voice with him together and in collaboration with him. And then through time, collaborating with other creative minds and film critics and people that love films such as yourself, Kevin, where you kind of – you use those experiences to help yourself grow into the film person that you want to be.

Kevin: Yeah, it totally makes sense.

Haskins: That's one of my favorite things. The first time Kevin was ever on the show and you got to hear like the full EFG experience, like the way that we would – when we talked about Suicide Squad I think and we were not kind to that movie. Kevin was ... [Laughter]

Esquivel: No.

Haskins: I think he was a little in awe at how much we went for that film's jugular a little bit.

[Laughter]

Esquivel: Yeah.

Kevin: Yeah. You guys definitely go in. But that's kind of the fun about it. So again, to kind of divert really quickly and talk about your podcast. I think at this point in time, you kind of have a well-oiled machine. So I think specifically in terms of the podcast, how did you guys go from, "Hey, let's do a podcast," to, "Hey, this is how we're going to set up the actual show. We start out with what are you drinking and going into all the different segments." And even the characters and things like that.

Haskins: The characters – I cannot even begin to tap into my co-host's mind over there because I don't know where they come from. I don't know what – there's a frog now on the show. It's weird. I don't even know. But for me, the first episode of Epic Film Guys Podcast ever was me talking into my phone giving a review of Terminator Genisys. Justin wasn't on the show yet and there were no segments, there was no intro, there was no outro, there was no nothing. It was legitimately just a stream of consciousness from me for 40 minutes.

But then as I involved myself and got myself deeper and deeper into the podcasting community, listened to and learned what other people were doing, and read a lot. I read so much about getting started with podcasting and how to make a more viable product. Yeah, if you're going to record for a 60 to 90 minutes show, do you just throw 60 to 90 minutes of audio on people or do you break it up in different segments? Do you take breaks? Do you give a little interlude here, a little bit of an interlude there? And I really think you do. I really think that it really helps the presentation of the entire things.

And then of course Justin and I love craft beer. You mentioned, "What are you drinking?" So that was an easy segue for us to just start bringing up and talking about craft beer on the show. Then we had to throw a segment in for trailers and I had my segment where I rant about stuff and just all sorts of other stuff.

Justin, any insight you can give us on the characters? Please. I'm all ears.

Esquivel: I have no idea. I have no idea. There is no explanation for any of the characters that have come out on the Epic Film Guys Podcast. The Lisp was an entity all into itself. It has long gone. We hope he doesn't ever come for more than one reason.

Haskins: You hope he doesn't ever come back.

Esquivel: The I think came from – if I had to find the reason, probably from my escapades going down to the local Irish pub Ned Devines. He probably followed me home one time and then we kind of just – I don't even know. From there, that's history. But there is a frog, Epic Film Frog. There is a frog on the show. No idea. Things just happen on the show. It's literally like taking a step into fantasy land and whatever happens, happens. So I mean yeah, all in good fun, I like to say.

Kevin: Got you. I think that's really helpful for people that are coming up and putting together a podcast. Even with my show, I finally feel like I have found the formula in

terms of how I do interviews and structuring it, but it's one of those things where folks don't tell you, "This is what you should do." And I think like you were saying Nick, just reading, and doing your research. I listen to so many podcasts on film that you finally kind of find your own niche and your own voice within it. So I think that's great advice.

Haskins: You have to find your voice as a podcast. I've said it a thousand times, especially with film podcast because there are literally four and a half billion of them. You have to present and that's what I try to do on the show every single week when I edit the show, and when we put it together. I think that's what Justin brings to the table as well. We're not selling the movies we are reviewing. We are not selling what we are talking about. We are selling us. We are selling Epic Film Guys as a brand.

Like when you tune in, you're going to get ridiculous frogs and you're going to get us talking about genitals and you're going to get all sorts of other insane, crazy stuff. I mean OK, you're probably going to get some of it in some other places too, but our personalities – you got to sell who you are, not what you are doing. You can listen to a review of Infinity War. Everybody reviewed Infinity War. Literally, everybody. But it's why do you tune into one show versus another to listen to their Infinity War review?

Kevin: Yeah. No, it makes a bunch of sense. All right. So next question, if it's true that there are only 7 basic plots in the world, how do you keep a fresh eye for every movie that you see?

Esquivel: You know, for me, it's all about following the youthful creativity in filmmaking. I like looking at what the up-and-comers are doing. Of course, you can go and check out the new Scorsese, the new Spielberg film – but for me, it's these guys, these up-and-comers that have this creative fire inside themselves.

And of course there are so many stories that we've seen and that have already been told, but a fresh pair of eyes can reinterpret those stories and give us a fresh take on those stories and breathe new life into them. And I think that's where for me at least, it makes me feel like I'm fresh and I'm up to date. Because if you don't follow who is the up-and-comer, if you don't follow the little guy on the corner there that no one is talking about, you're never going to see the bigger picture. I like to say this to Nic a lot, unfortunately, we don't get as much time as we would like to to review a lot of smaller films, but you really have to have an open mind to all genres. Everything.

Haskins: Everything.

Esquivel: If you're just sitting there and you're reviewing the big budget blockbuster that's out that weekend, that's going to get old. Your eyes are going to be set on that type of movie and you're going to see movies in that way. So I mean for me at least, it's really just looking at the up-and-comers, the Indies, literally everything, every type of genre to keep myself up to par.

Haskins: I've long said that the most important aspect of any film is its creative team. Think about a genre film, think about a comedy film, they're all the same. They've literally follow the exact same plot structure for the most part like you can follow them like literally like clockwork. But the creative team, the writers, the director, the actors, the crew, they elevate something from fine or good to great.

One example I always love to use when I talk about this kind of thing is Old School. I love Old School. I think it is legitimately one of the most perfect comedy movies of the past couple of decades. It's not any different plot wise. Literally, the plot beats are exactly the same as any other comedy that has come out in the past couple of decades. But Vince Vaughn, Will Ferrell, Jeremy Piven, all of these guys one hundred percent bringing their A game! Todd Philips dials it all up to eleven. Every joke lands so well. I just love it. That's the effort that you need in any kind of a film because yeah, there aren't really that many different variations you can go to in a plot. You're going to see the same basic story when you break it down to its nuts and bolts. But you just got to go old school in it. That's all it is.

Kevin: All right. So what advice would you have for the up-and-coming critic?

Esquivel: I'll go before Nic because I know he is going to have a long-winded response because he is the one who does all of the work. Above all this, even above doing the videos that we started with our YouTube and above doing the podcast, Nic can write reviews. He is a well-written critic as well. But I always come at it as you can't look at it as a chore, or as a job. It has to be your passion. It's more than just a hobby but what you live for because we live film. We love it. We have our passions. Everyone loves something whether it may be sports or you love craft beer or you love – it can be a lot of different things. But for me, it has always been music and film.

So I never let it be something that I don't look forward to. It has to be film equals life. And for me, part of that is the excitement of knowing that when I go to see a new movie, so for example, upcoming Deadpool 2, we're going to see that movie. We're not going to tell each other what we think about the movie until we actually sit to review it. So it will be exciting because who knows what the other person is going to say and what kind of information is going to get sparked in the conversation. So for me it has got to be your passion. It's got to be something you love. It's got to be something you want to do every single day. It's got to be something that you live and breathe.

Haskins: Mine is actually really, really simple. Own it. Be you. Stand by in who you are, what you believe, what you like. I've been straight-trashing the Predator franchise for like the past month and a half ever since this Predator movie has been in talks. Number one, because I know it irks Justin when I do it.

But number two, it's not me. I don't like it. So you got to own it. Just be who are. If you're honest, if you're straight up with your audience, if you give them you, if you just give them who you are, then they're going to respect you for it. If you're one of those people who just changes your opinion at a drop of a hat just to not have the debate or whatever then nobody is going to take you seriously. No one is going to care what you have to say. So be you. Own it. Own your words.

Kevin: Sweet. All right.

Haskins: Also, Predator sucks.

[Laughter]

Esquivel: I'm going to kill you. I'm going to kill you. You have no idea what's going to happen to you.

[Laughter]

Kevin: Why is the film critic important? On the flip-side, are film critics important?

Haskins: Definitely yes. One hundred percent yes. I think it's important for the same reason that education and critical thinking are important. And I would say even the most popcorn of popcorn films have layers and subtext in them. I think it's our responsibility as film critics to pull that kind of thing out and shine a light on it and put it out there for somebody else who is getting into film criticism. They can pull out our paper or podcast or and they could find out about it.

It's simple to go in and be like, "I like that person's performance. I didn't like that person's performance." But why? Why did it make you feel that way? What about that film got inside of you and provoked your passion? Or in some cases, it provoked your outright anger and hatred. How did it connect to you?

And I think it's important because criticism dissects the why of everything. Why was I entertained? What spoke to me? That's really all I can say about it. It's what about it gets in and connects with you. It's not just – like I said, I don't think it's – I think it's too superficial and too overlooks too many things I'll say to just say, "Oh, I like it. I like the explosions. They were good." [Laughter] Why? What did that make you feel? How did that make you feel? Get into it. Get into the heart of the matter. I think that's why criticism is important.

Esquivel: And for me, I think that cinema, film, movies in general, they're born to be talked about, breathed in and ingested into your being. I mean everyone takes a movie differently. They find their own experiences in the film with the characters they are watching on screen. And I think it's our natural reaction as human beings to react to that and to discuss it among peers and like-minded people.

And I think that a film critic is important because it creates that discussion. And the best filmmakers are making those films that we're watching to create that discussion. They want people to talk about their movie. They want it to be more than just, "I liked it." More than just, like Nick just said, more than just "yeah, those explosions were cool and I like when the robot punched the other robots through the building." I mean it really needs to be bigger than that.

And without film critics, without their insight, without them stirring the pot and getting their word out there, you might not know if a film is for your or it's not for you. Maybe because of their word, you're going to go see a movie because you disagree with them or you agree with them. And just like any other critic of any other medium, but I think for film especially, it's something that again, because so many people can watch a film, five different people can watch a film and each one of those people are going to take away something differently from it. And I find that to be extremely interesting and I like hearing people's thoughts on that.

And there are those critics that certain people will connect to and you're always going to go by that person. You may not always agree with them but you're always going to know that you can trust them. And I think that that's the opening of the gates so to speak into the film world for some people and I think it's extremely important. Without film criticism, I don't think film would be nearly as successful as it is.

Kevin: Sweet. Last question guys. Where do you see film criticism headed?

Haskins: I see it headed downward in some ways. I think that the rising prevalence of sites like Rotten Tomatoes and the importance of a Tomatometer or an aggregate scorer versus the actual ratings of the film, skews audience perspectives. And I think it's a disservice to one critic's thoughts about any particular film because all it does is aggregates whether your review is positive or negative and spurs it into a percentage.

Think about how many times you've heard that, "Oh, the film is certified fresh. It has a 100% and 99 and 98% rating on the tomato meter." So it gives the audience out there a perception that this film is perfect or it's near perfect when in reality, it's an aggregate of 157 out of 10 ratings. They're all positive ratings. They're mostly positive ratings but they also all had serious issues with the film. But it gets that 99% stamp because it's a "passing grade."

The same happens with movies with lower Tomatometer scores. If you get something that's a 15 or a 20 or a 25, it makes you think it's completely devoid of any kind of merit. It must completely terrible. It must be one of the most abominable pieces of garbage that has come out in cinemas in a decade! However, what it is, is it's a bunch of mixed reviews. Some were extremely negative, some were extremely positive. But like I said overall, it just deludes a critic's value and words down into nothing. It's deluding you down into a piece of a percentage; it's a piece of an aggregate score.

And studios, of course, love it because if they get that certified fresh rating or if they get that high percentage, that's insanely good marketing. Better marketing than they can't even dream up in an entire marketing campaign for a film. Negative Tomatometer scores and things like that, can have the same kind of affect. As critics, the kind of crappy thing about it is, we're forced to go through these avenues. We're forced to be aggregated if we want to have a voice. But at the same time, it's just deluding us out. I barely gave it a recommendation, it was a six [out of ten], and I had a lot of serious issues with it. Yet that six is turned into a fresh score.

I think that's a very important distinction to make and I think that the longer that sites like Rotten Tomatoes have the prominence that they do, the worse it's going to get.

Kevin: Justin, you got any thoughts?

Esquivel: Well, where do I see film criticism heading? I think that – well, this is just me being completely frank review and honest, I think that a lot of people think they're critics. I mean everyone thinks they're critics. To be fair, we are. I mean you go to the local restaurant, you have a burger and if it's not good, you say, "I really don't like this burger." And some people will elaborate on to why they don't like the burger and they may get into detail.

And this continues to grow and grow with the advancing technology and especially social media. I can't remember the last time I went through my newsfeed on a given day without someone talking about a show, or a movie, or like I said a restaurant they ate at, or the concert they just went to.

Haskins: Politics. Anything.

Esquivel: Everything. And so, everyone is criticizing everything. It's literally now, with social media platforms out there, I think everyone may not necessarily think of themselves as a critic but they are acting out as such. It may not necessarily be in the most sophisticated way or the most organized way. I think it's very congested at this point.

That's not to put a damper on or to hate on anyone that's trying to actually be serious about it. I know those of us that do this, that they really put a lot of pride into it and put a lot of effort into it and think very seriously of it, there are people that just think "Hey, I'm just going to give this movie a rating. I'm just going to write a little mini blurb about it and I'm a critic." And that's not necessarily the case in my opinion. I still look back, Kevin, to the great critics and even the ones I disagreed with. Like when I grew up, I watched Siskel and Ebert all the time. I always completely disagreed with them when I was a young kid and I didn't understand why these guys, "Why are you hating the movie I just went to see that I love?"

But they were those people that you looked up to and you appreciated. Over time, I learned to appreciate them even more. I kind of get Nick's point about being disappointed about Rotten Tomatoes. I still look at it and I'm still that guy that gets really interested to see what the Tomatometer is going to bring especially upon this recording. I went and looked at what the Solo : A Star Wars Story reviews were hitting at just because I still like to look.

I hope that it gets more even in the way that it is portrayed and not so – it's not really fair to the movie sometimes. Sometimes it's not deserving. For a lot of the movies where I'm like, "What? This is getting this? Really?" But it's all personal opinion, and that's what it comes down to. I think that people sometimes forget that. It's all subjective.

Someone can go in and watch Black Panther and love it and think it's the best thing in the world and someone also can say, "Hey, I liked it for what it was but it wasn't for me." Both opinions are fine. Sometimes in some circumstances, there's not one right and one wrong. Sometimes there is. It comes down to what do you have to bring to the table in your criticism of what you're discussing? Have something interesting to say, and bring something new to the table. Like what Nic was saying earlier about what we do with our show, be yourself. Sell yourself and not really the film you're talking about. Do it in a way that you enjoy, you have a passion for, and do it with originality.

CHAPTER 7

JASON FRALEY

Name: Jason Fraley

Medium: Radio, Online, Television

Outlet: WTOP, thefilmspectrum.com

Years active: 12

Top 3 movies: The Godfather, Vertigo, It's a Wonderful Life

Favorite Director: Alfred Hitchcock

Jason Fraley is hailed by The Washington Post for “his savant-like ability to name every Best Picture winner in history”. He began at WTOP as Morning Drive Writer in 2008, then became the station’s film critic in 2011 and eventually Entertainment Editor in 2014, providing daily arts coverage on-air and online. At WTOP, Jason won a regional Edward R. Murrow Award for his feature behind the music of “La La Land,” a Society of Professional Journalists award for his “Gravity” review and an Associated Press award for his feature “Keeping the Drive-In Alive.” His list of celebrity interviews is endless, from red carpets with Steven Spielberg, George Lucas, Bill Murray, Eddie Murphy, Jerry Seinfeld, Julia Louis-Dreyfus, Tom Hanks and Morgan Freeman, to one-on-one chats with Aretha Franklin, Berry Gordy, Carol Burnett, Glenn Close, Pink Floyd, The Eagles, Robert Duvall and Jon Stewart, not to mention backstage interviews with Leonardo DiCaprio at the 2016 Oscars and Emma Stone at the 2017 Oscars.

In his spare time, Jason dabbles in filmmaking, having written six feature-length screenplays, including his debut "Cinemagic," which made the Top 10% of the Academy's Nicholl Fellowships. He has also directed several shorts in film festivals from New York to Chicago to New Mexico, including "Liberty Road," which won a prestigious CINE Golden Eagle Award.

Jason and I met at American University in the graduate film program. It was a really random meeting. It was one of those, "I've heard everyone mention this guy but I don't know him and we don't have classes together" type of things. We finally met in person when he assisted our television studio class project, called "Metro Monsters". He and I hit it off quickly and have been thick as thieves ever since! Jason loves the craft of filmmaking and probably loves talking film just as much. Same here. So it's no surprise that this interview went long, but his passion for the craft jumps off the page as you read it. This is a great look into how the examination of cinema can shape your understanding, develop your voice, and build your love for it!

Kevin: Jason, when did you first fall in love with film?

Fraley: Well, I have been obsessed with movies my entire life, pretty much as far back as I can remember. I mean my dad was a construction worker, my grandpa was a plumber, and of course they loved going to the movies but it wasn't anywhere in their realm to do something creative. I always had a theory that if I was an only child, I probably would have been in dad's hidden pocket learning that trade or whatever.

My theory is that because I was a twin – I have a fraternal twin, Josh, who lives in Frederick – the two of us were always off wandering doing creative stuff. We also spent a lot of time with our grandparents too. Even before we knew how to write, I remember standing at the typewriter, dictating to my grandma who would type these stories for us and we would make books. I would be the author, my brother would be the illustrator and we would always be doing something creative.

One of those things we would make were movies, probably around age – let's see, I was born in '84, so around age 6. You already know the story, but [Laughter] we went to see Home Alone at the movie theater. We were the perfect age for that because Macaulay Culkin was our age and it was a nice family movie but you still had some John Hughes script and Chris Columbus directing, now there is a little something there. It wasn't snowing when we went into the theater but it was snowing when we came out so it was a magical little Christmas movie as a kid.

Anyway, we raced home to my grandparents' house and made our own version called Boy By Himself, which was a great hilariously original title off of Home Alone and the plot basically consisted of me breaking into my brother's house, which was actually my grandparents' house. My grandpa filmed it – our Pap Pap. He had one of those big VHS camcorders. You had to slide a big tape in on your shoulder. He would film it. My grandma did some very amateur acting as the, "Oh my God! We slept in. We're late to the airport. We left our son at home." Not winning any Oscars. [Laughter] Maybe some Razzies for that performance but love grandma, love my Mee Maw.

I mean it's wild to think back then. You had to edit

everything in camera. We didn't have Final Cut Pro or anything. You would have to shoot shot by shot after he would hit record, you act out the scene – kind of improv it a little bit – and then we would flash a peace sign at the camera saying cut to our grandpa. We would make like a little scissor motion with our fingers saying cut and he would cut and then we would do the next scene together.

It was a very green amateur way but like I feel like even before we knew how to really read and write, we were already kind of learning these beautiful concepts of this whole language of movie making. I mean we were just doing it for fun.

So yeah, so there was the Home Alone thing and then from there, you're kind of hooked. I'd say like most kids growing up in the '80s and early '90s, you start falling in love with all the blockbusters of I'd say the three main ones at that time: Steven Spielberg, George Lucas, and Robert Zemeckis.

Indiana Jones was my hero as a kid. I watched those movies over and over and over again. You'd see some making of stuff on Jurassic Park, Spielberg talking about the making of a movie, and you start to understand on a different level. I had the Star Wars bed sheets, although I was always more of an Indie [Indiana Jones] guy than Star Wars. Zemeckis with Back to the Future and Who Framed Roger Rabbit and Forrest Gump – he releases all of those right in my formative childhood years and I'm hooked.

Of course, The Wizard of Oz, I mean I wore that tape out as a kid. Then of course all the Disney movies too. Actually, I think the Little Mermaid was probably the first movie I actually went and remember going to because it would have been 1989. I mean we grew up on Disney movies but it's interesting that that was sort of the rebirth – I mean Disney animation almost shut down in the '80s. They're about ready to shut it down and then the Little Mermaid infused a new life – they were like, "Let's try making like a Broadway musical."

Then all of a sudden they went Little Mermaid and Beauty and the Beast, Aladdin, Lion King and then Toy Story came and I remember being like, "Whoa! What is this digital thing?" You could tell going to Toy Story that it was like our generation's Snow White. It was the very first feature of its kind and we were like, "Whoa!" All these things, I was just starting to geek out on and I always loved movies. Absolutely just from a pure fan point, from a pure popcorn nature.

Then of course you're a teenager so you're seeking out Tarantino's Pulp Fiction and Scorsese's Goodfellas, or the Christopher Nolan Memento and those kind of cool movies – the little edgier stuff that's pushing things a little bit. So you're starting to understand on a slightly different level through your high school teenage years. Even in high school, we played sports and all the usual jock stuff, but then on the side we would go home and we would make movies. We made Indiana Jones spoofs Mel Brooks' style.

So we made movies all through my childhood, all the way through my high school years and then off in college. It became a more serious thing, which I think probably leads to your next question.

[Laughter]

Kevin: I appreciate that, Jason. I guess for the book, it should be noted that you are the savant and you know all of the best pictures from 1929 or what is it, '28?

Fraley: Yeah. The first two years were a double year. So it was like '27, '28.

Kevin: Right.

Fraley: The first one, yeah. Oh, and I'd like to make an amendment. I would also like to drop in there that I loved Rocky as a kid, playing sports and stuff. So that was one of the other formative ones. But who didn't? [Laughter]

Kevin: Yeah, no doubt. All right. So the next question is: what drew you to the art of film criticism? So obviously, we all fell in love with movies at a young age but then there's this art form to actually critiquing a movie. So, what drew you to the art of film criticism?

Fraley: Basically, everything I just described to you was how I fell for movies on just a pure fan level as a kid, like we all do. Just sort of that magic experiential thing of watching movies that I'm going to love until the day I die.

But it wasn't until college that I started appreciating it as an art form. I guess the thing for me would have been when I went to do journalism at the University of Maryland as my undergraduate degree. I thought I was going to be a sports writer so I was just taking a bunch of journalism classes. On the side, I had to make a minor, and I had always loved movies so I took a film theory class and the professor was this older gentleman with a mustache named Joseph Miller. The class you go to is sort of in a stadium style seating at University of Maryland. It's a bigger campus. The first two hours of the class, he'd show a classic movie and then the last hour, he would go up to the front of the room and ask you about what you just saw thematic-wise and plot-wise and all that – commentary-wise.

What I really dug into – he would break down with freeze frame, shot by shot, what a strong filmmaker would do. He sort of taught us all the idea that there are regular ho-hum transparent filmmakers and then there are the strong auteur filmmakers that actually had – I don't want to call it a hidden agenda – something else symbolic going on under the surface that you could paint almost a whole separate story. Or in the best cases, a visual story that supports the actual written story just by how characters are grouped together. If they have a half-lit face – that means they are a dual persona or maybe evil – or if you have them behind sort of jail bar patterns of either window blinds or a fence – sometimes that can mean they are going to be doomed. Or just the angle, who has the power in the shot – whether you're looking up or down at someone – how they are grouped together in shots, the colors of the costumes, etcetera.

He started pointing out all of these things and my mind was really blown, like my noodle was cooked. I was in awe and I was like, "This is an art form. This is its own and I think it's the best art form." Because it combines photography, theater, literature, music, literally – painting, I think it combines all of them. When done really well, I think it's the ultimate art form.

So, I have to remember what we watched in that class – I know Citizen Kane and Cool Hand Luke and all the classics. But I remember my epiphany moment was when he showed John Ford's The Searchers – which the first time you're watching it, I thought it was just like any cowboy and Indian movie that my grandpa would watch with us on a Saturday. I thought it was fun and entertaining ride, like The Duke. It was fun – him saving Natalie Wood.

But then when the professor got up there and just breaking

down the first 10 minutes, there is this whole other movie at play. I mean not only in the title – he is a soul searcher going on this very-ahead-of-its-time study of racism and prejudice. This is pre "I Have a Dream"– this is 1956. So this is before To Kill a Mockingbird or anything where Ethan Edwards is battling these inner demons and by the end we try to see if he can overcome his prejudice towards Native Americans – which is something we're still talking about in this town of D. C., with sports teams.

But more importantly on the visual side, there was this whole love affair that John Wayne's character was secretly having with his sister-in-law, Martha – the one who is murdered by Comanches and then they steal the niece and everything. There is this innuendo based on how John Wayne and Martha are always grouped together in the shots or they reach their hands and touch a candle together, whereas her actual husband is always shown in a one-shot.

They are always together as a two-shot. At the end of the night, the husband and wife go into the bedroom together and John Wayne has to sit outside on the porch looking in through the frames within the frames of these brick walls. He has to go out on the porch with the dog out in the wilderness looking in through these frames within the frames and the theme is "What makes a man to wander, what makes a man to roam, what makes a man to leap, bend, and board and turn his back on home?" It's everything.

So anyway that made me be like, "Well, OK. There's a whole other thing." And then of course Citizen Kane and you start to realize the depth of field or that Charles Foster Kane walks deep into the background and visually gets smaller and then suddenly when the power turns in the scene, he comes back and walks towards the foreground and he is getting large again. Suddenly, I started to realize like, "Oh, I haven't even been watching movies close enough in the past." I was just looking for the plot and the entertainment value. Which you have to do on first watch.

I suddenly started to appreciate the notion that I don't think you can really call something a great movie or a masterpiece until you've seen it more than once. And that's when I fell for the art of it. I took seven more classes with the same professor, and each would be devoted to a different filmmaker. There's a whole class on Alfred Hitchcock, a whole class on Woody Allen, there's a whole class on whatever. And we would really drill down into their consistent auteur staples. I wrote a big final term paper on Rear Window all about how as James Stewart looks from window to window – it's a big metaphor for the filmmaking process and how the director cuts from shot to shot. That's Jimmy looking from window to window.

And I remember the professor called me in and I'll never forget his office. He had a big blue velvet poster on his wall. [Laughter] I went in and sat down and he was like, "This Rear Window paper is this is really something. You should go study in grad school." So I did at AU and the rest is history. But let's cut this question off and go to the next one.

[Laughter]

Kevin: All right, Jason. So how did you find your voice as a critic? Because I think that's one of the hard things to do. A lot of times there are so many different voices. You try to emulate a different voice when you first start out but eventually, you kind of settle on your own. So, how did you

find your voice as a critic?

Fraley: Well, I mean I definitely read a lot of reviews from all the great critics, from Roger Ebert to Pauline Kael. One of my mentors, Michael Sragow, who was the film critic up at the Baltimore Sun when I interned there. We thought Elizabeth Taylor was going to die so he tasked me with putting together a tribute montage and gave me a list of her movies. And I fell for A Place in the Sun and Giant and all these great George Stevens' movies – which is wild because a few years later, I interviewed George Stevens Jr. who founded the AFI and the Kennedy Center Honors, about Giant. So that was a wild turn of events there.

I would get all of their theories – like Pauline Kael said that she never watched a movie more than once. I remember she famously panned the Sound of Music and there were a couple of movies that turned out to be classics that she panned. She said she never watched it more than once. The more I looked into it, I respected her as a critic but I vehemently disagreed with that. I think it should work on first viewing but I think it absolutely should hold up and review itself as even greater on repeat viewings.

I think that started to get my voice where I thought movies should work as art and entertainment along a spectrum – along the "film spectrum" which is sort of a phrase I coined in a website I made – where I actually think it's lazy if you make a movie just for the mainstream audience. Of course, if it's just a big blowup blockbuster special effects thing like Transformers and there are no other symbolic layers or subjects, I think that's lazy. You're only going half of the pathway.

What might be contrarian to film scholars – and I don't care but I'll say it – is that it's lazy if you're just working on the symbolic levels and the artistic levels but it's not accessible to an audience. I think you're also maybe not so lazy but you're not doing as well as you could because why not try to reach the widest audience ever? That's why I love the Hitchcocks and the Billy Wilders and the folks like that – they aren't masterpieces made under the guise of mainstream entertainment. That's really what I started appreciating.

Honestly, the real thing that honed it was in college and in grad school – mostly in undergrad – I printed off every best list possible, Time Magazine, AFI Top 100, Entertainment Weekly, Sight & Sound Magazine. I mean this is the turn of the century around the millennium so everyone is putting up a best list. With a highlighter I went down one by one and had a notepad and a pause button on my remote at home and watched every great movie ever. I took really in-depth, copious notes on all the symbolic imagery that I was finding that I had been equipped with from these film theory classes with Joseph Miller.

I wanted to take it to the next step and say, "All right. What makes a great movie great? There has to be a secret here." So I took it upon myself when no one else was looking, other friends would be going out – I still did the social thing, play flag football and whatever. I would make time to run to the library and on LaserDisc or DVD or VHS. In one case, I watched Duck Soup on a two-reeler and I was like, "What makes the great movies great?"

So I went through all these lists. I took spiral notebook after spiral notebook and then I eventually wrote them – I sat down and just started typing out reviews. I wrote that 300 in-depth analyses on all these classic movies and I wasn't sure if I was going to start a book or a website but I eventually put them into a website called the Film Spectrum. I think only about a hundred of them got posted before I got the [W]TOP gig so there's a whole stash of 200 classic movie reviews that I never posted, just sitting at home – I might get them up there someday.

But to answer your question, I think that's what honed it – just hammering away at it, asking that inquisitive question, "What makes a great movie great?" Then putting the brain muscle behind it and trying to figure out all these symbolic tricks and auteur staples that they had, take all these notes, write it out and then the more you write, the more you hone your voice. Even if it's for a blog, that's what I tell everyone to do – just do it. You have to just get out and do it and just bang away at your craft.

Kevin: If it's true that there are only 7 basic plots in the world, how do you keep a fresh eye for every movie that you see?

Fraley: I actually think that's one of the hardest parts of the job because a lot of audience members or even newer critics who don't have a basis of knowledge of film history. I think they see something and they say, "Oh, that's great. That seems so original." But if you have seen all these movies and can memorize all the dates like I can, because I sat and hammered away at all these reviews and memorized the dates and the storylines and plots and the directing and everything that has come before in the arc of movie history. If you look at it from that standpoint, the stuff that other people might find original, you're not really finding that original because you've seen it before.

I really do think that's the most challenging part of the job.

Even on a week-to-week level, so much of it has to do with what you just saw before. If you saw something amazing the week before then the next movie you go and review you're holding it to that standard and it's just kind of pale in comparison or vice versa. If you saw something that was pretty crappy the week before, then you might even have a tendency to overrate the movie you see the next week.

So I think that's the hardest thing especially the fact, like you mentioned, there are only 7 plots, which is fine. I don't think anyone should be dinged for recycling – there's only a certain amount of hero's journeys and Joseph Campbell and all that stuff that you can actually do. I don't necessarily want someone to totally reinvent the wheel but it's more of working within the frameworks of those existing character arcs.

How creative are you within that? That's what I'll reward.

Kevin: So if you could, how do you keep your eyes fresh? Every time that you walk into the theater, you say, "You know what? This is a new film. I'm just going to go blank slate and not judge it," because you've seen something like it before.

Fraley: Right. I think you just try to put to bed whatever you had just seen the previous week or day or whenever you saw your last movie, and you try to go in there clean slate. When those lights go down, try to treat it like a giant new eraser that wipes you down or a shower that wipes you clean and baptizes you in the magic of cinema and you're just going to sit there and try to enjoy it as a viewer would. That's what I always try to do, think about how someone off the street, they walk in and sit down. How are they going to experience the movie? That's sort of the entertainment accessibility side of it.

And while I'm doing that, I'm registering that as an entertainment ride. I'm trying to look for all the directing techniques and stuff that I've sort of trained myself – or that taking film classes has trained you to do.

But I think another thing is to just treat it like you're a mainstream moviegoer. That's why I try not to take notes while I'm in there. I did that the first few times and I realized really quickly that it wasn't like when I was checking off the best list at home and I could pause the movie. In the movie, if you try to do that and take notes, you're inherently missing the dialogue or you're missing a plot point because you're sitting there writing. Plus, you're in the dark so you can't really see what you're writing.

I just try to treat it as a moviegoer and just experience it, because there is a magic to movies sucking you in. The really good ones are suddenly over and you say, "Wow! Wait. Where did the time go?" It's usually the bad ones that you notice were sitting at the theater and look at your watch. It's going to happen. So I would say just treat it like you're a moviegoer going to watch it, how are they going to take it in? While you are doing that, start making mental notes of the art of it because film critics and academics and more cultured people who have seen a lot of movies and seen the previous iteration of whatever the story is will also be reading your reviews. You got to reach them too. So yeah, I think it's just trying to remember to balance.

Kevin: Yeah. I find it funny because as you were talking, I remember when I first started out in those days of actually carrying a little notepad and I don't do that anymore. I think anything that you continue to hone over time and keep hammering away at – eventually you get really good where

you can just take those certain notes in your head.

Now sometimes, I do. I'll have my movie ticket or something and I'm trying to jot something down because I think of an angle to kind of come at to review with. Or there was a certain thing that I want to make sure that I hit. But other than that, I think you're totally right. After doing it for such a long time, you start to just start writing in your head as you're watching. But definitely you got to get rid of the notepad and just kind of let it wash over you. But at the same time, you're writing the review as you're watching the film.

Fraley: Absolutely. I still do see a lot of critics in the theater who are very acclaimed and esteemed and have been doing it a while that still take notes and more power to them if they can do that. It's just not how I choose to work. I guess I just tend to have a photographic memory for some of the stuff or I can remember certain images or dialogue lines. I just make a mental note and then I still take it in as an experience and then right when it ends is when I go out – you'll see me probably staggering around, bumping into things in the lobby because I'm emailing myself notes. I immediately get out of the theater.

[Laughter]

Kevin: I have seen you do that. I remember that.

Fraley: Just get out of the theater. That's when I'm like, "Okay. Before I go to sleep and it goes away or even on the drive home, before I even do that I want to just get down in writing everything I just made mental notes on." But to me, that tends to work better than trying to take notes during.

Kevin: All right, man. So, what advice do you have for

the up-and-coming critic?

Fraley: Based on my own personal experience I would say hammer away on your craft when no one is looking. Be the Andy Dufresne behind the movie poster chiseling away at the Shawshank wall and no one is going to see that you're doing it. To continue the analogy, they're just going to see the Andy Dufresne out in the prison yard, a.k.a. whatever you're doing on your daily job for work or school or whatever.

But when you're in your spare time, set your alarm clock. I remember setting my alarm clock for 5 AM because I heard that High Noon was coming on Turner Classic and I had a reviewed to get, so I set my alarm and got up and drank coffee and wrote the review. In between classes or when your friends are getting ready to go off to parties but you want to go to the library really quick and take some notes on why Chinatown was great or why Fargo was great, whatever it is. Just do it. Make the time to do it.

There are only so many hours in a day and everyone else that's lazy is going to take the lazy way out, so be better than that. Even if it's just an hour or two a day, eventually this will add up and you'll be way ahead of everyone and you remember the movie dates and suddenly they'll call you a savant but it really was just hard work.

[Laughter]

Kevin: I love that.

Fraley: Honestly, that's all I would say. I mean a great starting point is printing off a best list and just going down it one by on and then rent those movies. Everything is at our fingertips now. You can find it all in streaming or on-demand now. You don't even have to go to the library like we had to do.

So just go down. Ask that question,"What makes the great movies great?" Make it a big mystery for yourself, a big challenge. Figure out the secret and eventually, you'll start noticing – you'll start figuring out the answer. Just take notes and then start writing. Like I said, make a blog. You can do it for free – make a website. Start writing and start putting them together because then I would say when opportunity meets preparation is when there's success.

So just start doing it. Don't be like, "I want to be a movie critic. How do I start?" And look at job postings because I hate to break it to everybody, it doesn't really exist. A lot of people do it for free or maybe very little money as just a side gig in addition to their day job. I guess my other advice would be to just get your foot in the door at some publication. I mean that's what I did at WTOP. I was the news writer from 4 AM to noon just writing news copy while building The Film Spectrum, while getting my Master's in Film at American University. By the time– it was a crazy, fortuitous event, but our movie critic, Joe Barber, wound up passing away which was horribly sad – he was a great guy.

The point being is when that opportunity came up, everyone in the newsroom already knew I was this huge movie buff. They would call out movie dates and I would yell out the best picture and then I would go back to my day job. But the thing is that you can make your life into what you want it to be. All it takes is just dedicating the time and the work ethic to do it.

And then suddenly, I think the universe sort of pays us off. It's like the karma thing. You know what I mean? I think if you wanted something bad enough and you're sitting there putting in the time or if you're Rocky pounding on the meat and running through the streets of Philly in the morning with that great Philadelphia morning theme by Bill Conti– eventually, the universe will bend in your direction and suddenly an opportunity will open up and you will be ready. You will be ready to go. So I guess that will be my advice.

Kevin: Jason, I think this has been the film nerdiest interview [Laughter] thus far. But I love every single second of it. That Shawshank will–

Fraley: Good luck combing through it all.

[Laughter]

Kevin: I know. That Shawshank metaphor was on point. I love it. I think that's great advice. So we got two more questions.

Fraley: Yeah, yeah. We'll keep it quick.

Kevin: Why is the film critic important? Perhaps the question could be, is the film critic important? Maybe we're not. But why?

Fraley: I would like to think it's important, or else why are we doing it? Other than we love it I guess. I think it's important I guess sort of big picture and more small picture – the macro and the micro, the anthropological reason and then the everyday person life. I think that it's important for both.

I think in the big picture, I think we're sort of the cultural gatekeepers. We get to help decide what work of art and entertainment is culturally significant. The movie that the National Film Registry will 25 to 50 years from now will look back and add to the registry as culturally important. We got to kind of see that on the cusp, in real time and our year-end best list and our star ratings and rankings and everything like that. What we predict is going to win the Oscars. In real time, we are getting to put those dots in the arc of movie history. If you view it as a big ongoing arc, I think it's fun that we get to put the dot on that arc.

I think that's a thrill because those are the cultural markers that years from now, people will look back and it helps distill in a time capsule of what that time period was about. And of course, the great movies are usually ahead of their time. So it's up to us to figure out what's ahead of the time while we experience it in real time – to me that's the magic. We are experiencing these movies in real time as they are coming out – actually before they come out, a lot of times – and then trying to predict what actually is ahead of its time. That's really exciting, the cultural gatekeeper.

On the small level, it's the service or the actionable information you're providing to who, in my case, the listener or the reader or the viewer is. Everyone has a short attention span now. We are inundated with so many great TV shows and movies and it's just giving them advice on what to spend their hard-earned money on, and shooting straight with them. I think that's the importance of a critic – to not talk over people or not talk down to people. I have a pet peeve – if ever I read a critic that's sort of snobby and seems to get off on bashing the movie, it's like, "What have you ever made movie-wise?" I think of that scene in Birdman when Michael Keaton calls up the theater critic in a bar.

But also from a helpful standpoint, what good are you doing to a reader if you're just bashing something? What good are you doing to help them decide what movie to go see that weekend?. I think it's good to point out the merits and the flaws, the good and the bad in everything and try to give constructive criticism and critiques rather than bashing or on the other hand, blind praise – explain why that is. Educate the reader a little bit, but educate them in a way that's conversational and colloquial.

In fact, I would just use the word conversational because colloquial isn't conversational.

[laughter]

Big picture: cultural gatekeepers; small picture: help the young couple going on a date or the family that wants to go out or the simple guy who wants a night of escapism. Help them decide what they should go spend their hard-earned money on.

Kevin: All right. The last question is: where do you see film criticism headed?

Fraley: I think that's such a fascinating question because I think – especially in the 21st century and especially now with Rotten Tomatoes – everyone could be a critic now, which I think is a double-edge sword. So on the one hand, everything is being democratized, anyone can be a critic, which is great for some things. Everybody's voices can be heard and that's going to lead to a more diverse group of opinions. People are going to be able to analyze movies no matter where they live or their station in life, and I think that's great.

The danger that I see is that we sort of have this cacophony of voices of everyone just sort of stalling off. I guess if everyone considers that all of those voices are equal – and I guess all the voices are equal, everyone's opinion matters. That's for sure.

I guess what I'm getting at is that I worry that maybe there are other younger critics out there that are not as knowledgeable and schooled in film history. It doesn't mean they have to go to film school. I mean it definitely helps if you can. Teachers will help you have epiphany moments like I did. But like I was saying, you can literally just sit at home with the best list and stream the m so you don't need to go to film school.

I hope that with the democratization, I hope it's in incumbent on all of these up-and-coming film critics to do their due diligence and get caught up on all the classics before they go out and start reviewing stuff.

So in terms of loads of trends, I guess I worry about the franchise model. A lot of the superhero movies have sort of set the stage for that – you always feel like you're dropping in on chapter 7 of the story rather than the origin story or the self-contained story where you get to see the hero gain his powers and then Michael Keaton defeats the joker and then the movie ends. That's why a lot of times now, it's just a set up for the next one and as a critic that I think the future of criticism is almost daunting because movies themselves are almost like TV shows now, where it's all serialized and it's not one long on-going story.

I actually have a quote for you. I'll read it to you, Kevin. I interviewed the Directors of Avengers: Infinity War, Joe and Anthony Russo and he had a fascinating quote but it also gave me some pointers about just where we are now. He is talking of Avengers the whole Marvel model and he said, "It's a grand experiment in narrative. Two-dimensional 2-hour close-ended stories had an incredible run for about a hundred years but I think audiences are interested now in storytelling that takes place over several years and several films. You can sit around, decrying the demise of the daguerreotype or you can look toward the future. Technology has altered this generation significantly and the way they process and consume story is now different."

And on the one hand, it's true. You have to embrace technology and changing terms and you definitely don't want to sound like, "Get off my lawn." You want to embrace trends, technological trends and audience trends. But the part that I vehemently disagree with – and please put in the book – [Laughter] is that, with all due respect to the Russos, I've enjoyed a lot of the Marvel ones too. I think the idea that "two-dimensional 2-hour close-ended stories had an incredible run for a hundred years but now it's time for something different" – I disagree vehemently.

I mean, I think the self-contained, close-ended story is what makes movies different from TV shows. If we're going to make the big screen experience the same as a TV series with all these episodic installments then what's the difference? Why should people leave their houses? You know what I mean? So I think for the health of the industry, I think we should latch on to the self-contained 2-hour story as what differentiates it from TV.

To me, that's where I'll disagree with that. Technological changes are great and all but I really miss the self-contained story because that itself is an art – that's screenwriting. That directing where you know where it's going to end and you have to come to a closure. Then you can plant all the breadcrumbs and symbolic directing and little red herrings and everything. But everything that gets you there to that final closure moment – I miss that closure. Talking about where the future is going, I sit there and think about how I fell in love with movies by highlighting and checking off all these best lists.

But the future of us critics now are, “How do we take this Avengers model and which one goes on the best list?” They’re all pieces – you put together the whole thing, that’s almost not even fair. That’s like 28 or a 30-hour movie. That’s where I sort of disagree. I’m definitely old school. But the open-ended episodic franchise installments – I think they should stand on their own. Let’s say The Dark Knight. I could see that making the best list going forward if there is a list of a hundred best movies of the 21st century. That’s fine.

I often wonder if you’re not going to have Thor: Ragnarok or whatever the movie of the year is because that’s sort of where I kind of get off the train and start to worry. Every time I sit in the movie theater, I want that movie I’m sitting down to watch to have a chance of being on that next best list because that’s how I view it. I view it as the arc of movie history and I want it to make that best list. That’s what I had a hard time wrapping my brain around – “Which chapter of this do I put on the best list?” I almost want to dock a movie a half star or a star if it’s part 7 just right out of the gate. Maybe that’s not fair, but to me it’s not original.

I mean the original Star Wars deserves it or maybe The Empire Strikes Back or Godfather I and II if you want an example of actually good sequels. I feel like those movies will be on the best list 99% of the time over The Last Jedi just because they were the original cultural moment.

Or Jurassic Park: Fallen Kingdom, you go and review that and you try to enjoy that as an experience but you know that Jurassic Park is going to be the original – it’s going to be the one on the best list. So that’s the hard time I have and maybe it’s an open-ended answer to your question but I think that's going to be the challenge that critics working right now and especially in the future that we have to solve. We have to decide if we're going to hold those filmmakers and those films to that higher standard – which I think we should – and keep rewarding the original ideas like when a Get Out comes along or A Quiet Place or Tully – those are just on the top of my mind.

Black Panther – which I guess he had appeared in Civil War but it wasn't original. That was an origin story with a self-contained story – it's a great movie. So I still think as critics we need to be willing and daring to hold up those original ideas like Get Out. While we can still give a pretty good review to Infinity War, we can say, "It's a good movie. Go see it as a fun experience that summer." But I think we should always reserve our 4-star reviews and "That movie is a masterpiece" and that kind of thing. I think we should reserve those for the great new ideas like a Get Out. I think that's our job and our challenge going forward.

CHAPTER 8

TIM GORDON

Name: Tim Gordon

Medium: Television, Radio, Online

Outlet: filmgordon.com, 96.3 HD4, Around Town

Years active: 26

Top 3 movies: The Godfather trilogy, On The Waterfront, Rashomon

Favorite Director: Christopher Nolan, John Ford, Martin Scorsese, Francis Ford Coppola

Film Critic, Association President, Brand Creator, and lover of ALL things film, **Tim Gordon** remains a true cinema innovator. He began his career in 1992 as a film critic and in 2002, he was named President of Washington (D.C.) Area Film Critics (WAFCA). The 50-member association examines issues pertaining to critics throughout the industry, and they annually honor the year's best films and performances. Gordon created the movie brand, "FilmGordon" consolidating his film content and social media platforms under one umbrella in 2008 and joined the nation's largest film critics association, the 350-member Broadcast Film Critics Association (BFCA) in 2013. Currently, he hosts the weekly film show, Keeping It Reel with FilmGordon on 96.3 HD4 on DC Radio.

Tim and I have become great friends over the years since I became a member of WAFCA. I still joke about how I used to call and hound him about getting tea or coffee to chat about being a film critic. (That's a whole 'nother lesson.) If there's one thing about Tim that I've always admired, it's how he works a room. Whether we're at Sundance, Middleburg (Film Festival), a local theater, or grabbing a bite, he knows how to talk to people. It's like his super power. Tim isn't the guy that starts talking to a random stranger, completely oblivious to the fact that he's bothering them. Rather, Tim can connect within seconds and draw someone into a casual conversation. That sense of familiarity is something he infuses in his writing, as well as his radio show and television appearances. Combined with his knowledge of cinema and cinema history, Tim's passion for the craft and his ability to connect with people earn the respect of colleagues and listeners alike.

Kevin: All right, Tim. When did you first fall in love with film?

Gordon: Wow! I had a father who love films. [He] dragged me to the movie theaters at five. As far as I'm concerned, man, film has been woven into my DNA from the love my daddy had which he passed on to the womb to [Laughter] to me who just kind of like picked up the torch man, and kind of ran with it. So, I would say all my life man, I mean it's – film has been a constant. It's been like my companion throughout my entire life, man to be perfectly honest.

Kevin: All right.

Gordon: I'm sorry, I could give you more but I'm trying because I understand that you don't need me to give you a full hour of quotes. I'm quote machine so I can keep in going just let me know.

Kevin: How about this – do tell the story of your father bringing home the paper that had what was coming out.

Gordon: All right. My father worked at North Star-Ledger which would be the equivalent of like the Washington Post or any major newspaper. And I would spend hours, man, going to visit my father at work and going through the archives as they would probably be known now. And you know, falling in love with history and that sort of thing. Probably when I was a teenager, my father brought home a production book from MGM and this probably was like – and that was probably in the mid to late '70s. I had never seen anything like it before. Commonly now, we know when you look at Marvel, we chart out the MCU for the next 10 years. But we didn't have that 40 years ago, man.

So, 40 years ago, they would come out with these preproduction books. That MGM one that he gave me had movies five years in advance and it blew my mind man, because I was like, "Wow, man you're able to tell me that in [19]83 these movies would come out? In [19]82 these movies would come out?" So, it sort of solidified in my mind at that time that film – you know, my father used to tell me a lot of stuff about movies. He would tell me stuff like "if you ever saw how movies were made you probably would like them." And to a certain extent, I understand exactly what he was saying when you go back in and you see how movies are shot in front of green screens and actors are doing their stuff. Then you take CGI and you make movie magic.

Well, I would disagree with my father, not that I would not like movies if I saw how they were made but it gave me a greater understanding on what the craft is about. All leaves magnificent individuals who work behind the scenes in order to craft the stories and what we call movie magic that we see. But that was a turning point for me in my development as a person who will later end up being in film because it kind of showed – for me, it represented the possibility of what films were and like "wow, man there's actually a plan in place on how these things get made. There's a plan on how studios kind of like organize and you know buy books and buy the rights to books and then work in production with those books. Then cast the actors and find the director and all the people behind the scenes."

So, that's what film, that's what that moment as I've come to think of it now represented for me which I'm probably articulating for the first time because I'm talking to Kevin Sampson, because nobody else thought enough to ask that question, man. So, then you are the Oprah Winfrey of this thing, man. [Laughter] These scintillating questions, behind the scenes like, "Go ahead, Tim, cry!"

[Laughter]

Kevin: I'll take that, I'll take that, man. That's funny.

Gordon: [Laughter] Right.

Kevin: All right. So, next question is what drew you to the art of film criticism, right? I do feel like as critics, this isn't a job that you take because you're going to make the most amount of money or whatever but it's something that you really love. And so, what is it about the art of film criticism that drew you in?

Gordon: Wow, man that's – that's a really good question, man. You must be writing a book or something, man. This is good stuff. [Laughter] Ironically, I literally just told a story on Facebook a couple of days ago which is why it's perfect timing for you. I met Charles Burnett the first time. I'm going to weave the story back around the film criticism but I'm going to start some place else.

I don't get star struck by a lot of people because I've met a lot of people working in the radio and interviewing actors and filmmakers over the course of a quarter of a century. But I was humbled meeting Charles Burnett because of what he represented to me personally when I was a young pup in the game. And I wasn't even in the game yet but I remember watching The Five Heartbeats by Robert Townsend and watching Charles Burnett's To Sleep with Anger and being struck by how both those movies touched me and how they didn't kind of touch anybody else in the community. Those movies sort of kind of came and went- were little cult films – and then it kind of didn't resonate at all.

It touched me because those two movies led me to a series of examination of my life path. And I remember at that time watching those two movies and going "man, if these movies aren't connecting with the public I've got to do something about this." I had to figure out why that was. So, it spurred me to create a company called Third Renaissance, which at that time represented the third renaissance of African American film. You know, Oscar Micheaux and that period from the beginning to inception of film in 1949 being period one. The rise of Poitier in 1950 to 1985 representing the second renaissance. Then of course the rise of Spike Lee to the current day of where we are.

Along with creating Third Renaissance, I created a newsletter which I wrote reviews for the first time, along with a good friend of mine named Garfield Tyson. And we published that for like three or four years. That lead to me getting into radio, which led to me becoming a film critic, which led to me being the President of the Film Critic Association creating the Black Reel Awards, creating FAAAF, me joining the BFCA, and creating The Film Gordon brand. So, Charles Burnett is literally is the foundation of my professional career and his films. Not just that one but Killer of Sheep, and later on The Glass Shield.

So, this is a brother who literally just got his honorary Oscar last November at the Governor's Ball and I'm sitting and talking to him, telling him what I'm telling you. He got a little misty in the eye and thanked me for telling that story. I was like, you never understand the impact! Like Charles Burnett, I'm assuming made that movie right in 1990, '91 and then it was edited and put it in together. He didn't know the impact that what he was doing would have on people like me or like what somebody did that had an impact on you. So, we don't know in what we're doing you know between creating this book, you're doing the DCBFF, you got Picture Lock- you don't know who you are inspiring or touching.

So, it – we all pay it forward. We all have these moments, where the things that we do resonate and touch people. So, I'm just thankful, man. But how that informed my film criticism is that it taught me at a very early age to trusty my voice, right? I knew that I had to be authentic from day one and build credibility with an audience by being consistent in my convictions. You know, people ask me to this day, "when you see a movie you like, how do you know you liked that movie?" And I said, "Man, I know it sounds real simplistic but I could feel it in my gut. When I watch really good movies, my gut will tell me, literally, my stomach will tell me that I'm watching it before my mind resonates like I could feel a good movie."

Like, for example, I saw a really bad movie that I won't name last night that I went in to the theater fully awake and the movie knocked me out and put me to sleep. It wasn't that I ate before I went in there. It wasn't that I had the itis. It was just a really predictably, very poorly executed story. And your gut will tell you that too. So, you've got to learn trust your instincts and then you've got to use your voice and your voice has to be consistent. And when I say voice I mean your convictions and your beliefs. I'm wrapping all that in under the auspices of voice.

You got to use your voice man, and understand what you're watching and then you got to be consistent and honest and you also have to be flexible because there had been times that I've watched movies that didn't play well in theaters then I watched them at home at 2:00 in the morning, they're fantastic. It's just not a movie that works in the theater and I can name numerous movies that this happened. Like I watch it at home and go, "Man, this is way better than when I saw it in the theater." So, it is what it is, man. But it is a unique and it's a very interesting fraternity that we belong to.

But for me, I always respect people that I think really putting the time and actually watched movies. It's not just about having really good opinions, you got to have a foundation of experiences in understanding classic Hollywood with modern Hollywood to really understand that at its core, Kevin, there's really a limited amount of stories. And these stories have been regurgitated and remanufactured over and over and over for new generations, man. That's all it is.

Kevin: Tim, you know, I love this. First off, you had answered the next question and now, you're giving me the

jump off for the follow-up question. So, you just answered how do you find your voice as a critic with trusting your gut, being, honest, be flexible. So let's move to the next question. If it's true that there are only seven basic plots in the world, how do you keep a fresh eye for every movie that you see?

Gordon: Oh, that's easy. You keep a fresh eye. No, no, I'm not, I'm not being funny. But the reason why I said that question is easy is because I have an understanding from all the roles that I've had in film over the course of my career. And when I say all the roles, I'm a critic who looks at movies for award shows, and my own award show. I look at them for laughter. I look at them for when I teach film. When I'm breaking films down. I look at them when I'm curating films needed for my monthly series.

So, film as I said earlier in this piece, it's so much a part of my DNA. You know how when food goes into your body, right? And the food has to be broken down and then it has to go into so many different places to do so many different things. That's the way I look at films. Film to me is like a big piece of chicken. I look at it and chop them up and separate it by the leg, the wing and thigh, you know, what's underneath. So, the way I look at movies is that I know going in that [A] I've seen all these stories before. My challenge, when I start a watching movie, is how fast can I figure this movie out? The longer it takes for me to figure a movie out, the better the movie is.

The challenge to me, in watching modern filmmakers, and when I really know they're doing a good job, is when they can take a concept that we've already seen before and they can bring something fresh to it, to kind of make it it's own. You talk about certain actors like Denzel Washington, who has been relevant for 35, almost 40 years because he made solid choices. So, in this business man, the people who survived and who become the legends are the ones you who become the tried and true either by how they write or give us something that's memorable in their direction. Or composers who create these memorable, indelible scores and things that you like that stay with you.

Daughters of the Dust is a movie that a lot of people have never seen but Daughters of the Dust is a movie that I think is one of the most gorgeously – one of the top three photographed films that I've ever seen and that's a credit to Julie Dash and Arthur Jafa, who was the cinematographer. So, for me, movies are about folks who understand how to take things and make them so creative that they stay with you. These people are able to take the old and give us something new. That's basically what it is.

Kevin: So, what advice do you have for the up and coming critic?

Gordon: First of all, you have to see a lot of movies, man, I mean before you call yourself a critic. There's a list of [AFI] films, the 100 Essentials, you should start there.

I spent a lot of years studying movies on Turner Classic Movies. I just did. I would gobble up everything I could watch on TCM, especially over the summer, where they would do series like Summer Under The Stars every August and they would give you 24 hours of an actor. I watched films from Bogart and Gene Jones and character actors. I would just watch movies and devour them.

I love filmmakers, man. When you talked earlier about my favorite films. The films of Akira Kurosawa, Billy Wilder, John Ford, Elia Kazan, Vincent Minnelli and more are on my list. I mean I watched movies by filmmakers. And these are the films that were the basis back when Hollywood had the studio system. I understand why the studio system was not good. But in some cases, I think the studio system gave us the classic period of Hollywood. I'm kind of torn because I believe that there were so many classic movies that were created during that time period because the studio system was all encompassing.

So, think of Marvel today, right? What Marvel is doing is basically the studio system, right? To a lesser degree. [Kevin] Feige is the boss. He hires a bunch of writers who specifically work and write on films from the MCU. They find actors who appear in the same movies over and over. Then they just make different movies and plug people in. The only difference is that instead of plugging them in to original, new stories, they're plugging them in to a bunch of different films in the MCU. You see the success that Marvel is having incorporating something old and as I said earlier, turning it into something new.

So, it has become sort of like the reason why the MCU works a certain way. It is run as like an updated version of what Hollywood did 70 or 80 years ago. It's the same thing, bruh. And that's what I was telling you earlier about how every time we look at this game and think we're seeing new stuff, we're really not seeing new stuff. We're seeing old stuff, repurposed in a new way. It's the craziest thing that Marvel has been able to do and people think it's easy, but look at the struggles that DC is having trying to do the same thing. So, I think I answered your question, I think.

Kevin: [Laughter] The original question was what advice do you have for the up and coming critic? And I think you said see a lot of movies [Laughter] and then we went off on

this...

Gordon: See a lot of movies! There. See lots of movies, trust your voice, and be consistent. Because there's nothing worse than a guy that will tell me and you offline, "man, that movie sucked" and then meet the filmmaker and be like, "Man, your movie was the bomb!"

[Laughter]

Kevin: All right. So why is the film critic important?

Gordon: When I first got into the business, the film critic was important. I remember idolizing the Arch Campbells and the Roger Eberts and Gene Siskels and Janet Maslins and all these other giants in the game. But the game changed going into the 21st Century. Blogs and social media became prevalent. To me it's not about how important the film critic is for studios, right now. It's not about the voice of a film critic or how articulate a critic is. It's about how many clicks he or she has. So, that is a common problem that I talked to my folks across the country who are talking about these new sites that have popped up and have got the clicks but they don't know – I hate use the phrase – shit from shinola. They don't.

Then you got people like me just standing on this curb like "I'm just going to keep doing me." I'm going to keep running my site, doing the stuff I do in film, and continue to follow my discipline even if I'm like a dinosaur. But I don't know if the film critic is that important anymore, man. I have a first row seat on this because what I'm telling you is real inside stuff. Even dealing with the agencies we deal with, the only time they really care about you, and I'm talking about you as the film critic, is when November rolls around and it's time to start a voting on awards.

You don't hear from studios any other time of the year as it relates to anything we care about because they don't care. The only thing they care about is awards. It's all they care about. And embargoes, "don't say crappy stuff about our movies before we tell you, you can see it. "[Laughter] But I don't know if the critic is as important and I think studios have tried to devalue the critic for many years, man.

Moving forward it's going to be really interesting because with all of these delivery models to get movies out there, they need quotes and things of that nature to sell the credibility of said critic to the public. But you can't have it both ways. You can't want the quote of the critic and then spend 10 months devaluing the critic. So, that's a really good question man, I really don't– what was the original question? What was the value?

Kevin: Why is the film critic important?

Gordon: I think he is much less important than he was, when I first got in the game but he still has some level of importance because the studios need somebody to validate the films that come out every year. And they turn to us first or critics across the country first in order to do that before the Golden Globes and Academy Awards get underway as a part of their three prong system every year from November to March.

Kevin: Makes a lot of sense. That helps us flow right into the next question which is, where do you see film criticism headed?

Gordon: Oh, good question. You know much like I told people, we have to wait to see about the equality of women in film and the whole Me Too movement and how that's going to change the game. Film criticism continues to evolve because like I said, you are raising up a generation of people now who [A] don't watch enough movies, [B] that aren't really skilled and trained as writers and critics were when I came along. So the youth factor, those two things, plus you add social media into the mix and you get a bunch of people who are only interested in writing stuff to get clicks.

I don't know man. It reminds me a lot of the 2006 movie Idiocracy from Mike Judge where a regular average guy who's like a C student lives long enough to become the smartest man in the world because he came up at a time with standards and the standards continue to deteriorate around him. I'm fearful for what a film critic will represent in 20 years. I'm thinking that they will continue to churn out these really uber expensive movies that will be poorly executed, pretty to look at, but [the critics] won't say anything.

Either the film critic will be non-existent because they wont need a critic in order to validate a story anymore or the people who will eventually do this job will be so neutered that it won't matte. I mean there are movies that come out now like Black Panther. Black Panther is a fascinating case study, man, of so many different things that are both right and wrong with our industry. There's a story that came out by Scott Mendelson that Black Panther is what's right and wrong with Hollywood. And basically, what he said in this article is that over the course of the five weeks that Black Panther was out, there had been five or six different tent-pole movies that studios initially had on the schedule that was supposed to come out and Black Panther obliterated all of them.

And he's saying if Hollywood can figure out how to make one movie that can just blow everything out the water is like studios lost millions of dollars, Kevin, making Red Sparrow because you know, we got Jennifer Lawrence and we got this – and Black Panther destroyed Red Sparrow. Black Panther destroyed every movie. It was like this tsunami that ate up so many movies and that was like man, studio should be terrified that there's a film that could come out because they're thinking Black Panther that it – it didn't finish in like 95 to 235 million, it would have been a solid earner. It would have made this money but then it wouldn't made enough room for other movies. But it destroyed all those movies making 1.2 billion and nothing else they came out doing that time that it was out, even got its hand to being successful.

So, my point to you is, is that in thinking about movies like this man there are always these periods of evolution. There are these things that come along and one way or the other change the game. So, when you're thinking about the direction of film criticism, film criticism is just a part of the overall business as a whole. So, if you go back and study in time at the beginning of the game, film critics meant everything in the beginning. And from that high level or that high pedestal that we were on, they've been slowly chipping away at it to the point that we're now at. That pedestal might have been five feet high at the beginning; it might be a foot and a half high now. And they're still chipping at it, man, trying to devalue what you say about a movie like, "Hey man, don't listen to Kevin and Tim. Man, go out and see our little funky movie." [Laughter] So that's basically what the game is, man.

Kevin: So kind of wrapping it up, you just feel as though there's a silent war between studios and the film critics. They

need us for the validation. Really what it is, is clicks are the eyeballs on their movies, right? But what they really need from us is that trustworthy authenticity that we bring to our reviews. So, people most of the time when you do go to a certain critic to read their reviews it's because you trust their voice. You agree with their opinions for the most part or like you said, they're going to be honest.

Gordon: Man, that's just it. There's a level of trust.

CHAPTER 9

BEN KENDRICK

Name: Ben Kendrick

Medium: Online, New Media, Radio

Outlet: Screen Rant

Years active: 10

Top 3 movies: Jurassic Park, Me, Earl & The Dying Girl, Batman

Favorite Director: Steven Spielberg, JJ Abrams

Ben Kendrick is the publisher of Screen Rant as well as the site's head film critic, and he serves as the host of the Screen Rant Underground and Total Geekall podcasts. He is a member of the Denver Film Critics Society as well as the Online Film Critics Society - with work referenced, cited, or syndicated on CNN, Wikipedia, Huffington Post, Rotten Tomatoes, IMDB, Yahoo, and Business Insider, among others. Thanks to a background in fiction writing, Ben is drawn to films that make story and character a priority; however, that doesn't stop him from enjoying a range of Hollywood offerings, ranging from blockbuster action flicks to campy so-bad-they're-good B-movies.

If you read one of Ben's movie and TV reviews or news

pieces, you'll notice that he has an ability to write with such articulation while also not going over the reader's head. Finding the balance between writing a well-constructed piece that doesn't read like an SAT question can be a challenge, but Ben makes it look easy. This made it fascinating to talk with him about his process. On top of that, it was great to hear his advice for up and coming critics, because becoming a host of a popular podcast and head writer of a review site doesn't happen over night!

Kevin: All right, Ben. So when did you first fall in love with film?

Kendrick: I think I first fell in love with film when – and I have this on my bio at Screen Rant and I joke about it a lot – I went to a midnight screening of Indiana Jones and the Last Crusade when I was tiny. It was back when midnight showings were really special. There was a table with merch, so I got a t-shirt and a poster that I had to buy and it was this big event. I mean it was one of the first times as a kid that I was in a packed movie theater and everybody was super excited to see the movie.

And so, I think that movie has kind of a mix of action and adventure and supernatural stuff. That was one of the first movies that I remember really connecting with. And after the fact, wanting Indiana Jones' hat and going back and watching Temple of Doom and Raider of the Lost Ark. I really got enamored with my experience there and it spiraled into a wonder of movie magic, I would say.

Kevin: Awesome. All right. Going from that young kid that was enamored with Indiana Jones and the Last Crusade, what drew you to the art of film criticism? Because I think there is an art to it. It's more than just saying, "That

movie sucked or that movie was awesome."

Kendrick: Yeah, for sure.

Kevin: But what drew you to the art of film criticism?

Kendrick: Yeah. I always draw the distinction between armchair critics – kind of like La-Z-Boy critics who will see a movie and will be like, "I liked that" or "I didn't like that." But what I think really drew me to it – I studied journalism in high school and also in college. I started out as a journalism major and I ended up switching into Creative Writing and English. I always had an interest in expressing my opinions to the public in a way where I could see something and dissect it in a way that would help other people appreciate it better.

But I think it was really when I fell in love with writing– writing was always sort of my subject in school. I went and got a master's in Creative Writing in New York between 2007 and 2009. And during that time, I spent a lot of time workshopping my own writing and giving feedback on other people's writing. It really taught me to be very technical about, "Is this accomplishing what the writer is intending for it to do? Is it eliciting the themes or the emotion that this person is trying to convey?"

And so, that's how – it sort of backdoored me into film criticism because I started writing about movies. I have always been a comic book geek and comic book movies were becoming popular. I had a friend who worked at Screen Rant and that's sort of how I got folded into it. It ended up being a really well-suited space for me because I could sort of look at movies, maybe in a way that a lot of people don't, necessarily. And the way that I primarily tend to look at them is through story.

So visual storytelling and stuff isn't what I tend to focus on as a critic. I can appreciate the difference between a Kurosawa film and a Michael Bay film or something, but the technical aspect of filmmaking is not where I'm strongest as a critic. I think the value that I really brought and what made me useful in the realm of film criticism – actually expressing whether or not this artistic and subjective element of film was successful or not is my own background in writing.

So when I watch a film, I tend to really follow if the character is getting set up in a way that by the end of the film I feel like they've gone on a journey and they've changed in some way. Not that they have to change – but the movie, by the end, has instructed me in some way about this character that I feel closer to them or I feel what the filmmaker wants me to feel – whether that's closer to them or whether it's horrified by them – and those feelings are supposed to communicate something about life in some way or another. Whether it's a popcorn movie and those that communication is a little bit more shallow. Or whether it's a really rich and textured drama in which what it's trying to communicate about life and the world is the point of the movie. I think that's sort of the through line through which I really see film.

Kevin: Got it. So one of the things for me personally as I was trying to get into film criticism more as a profession – like we were talking about, there are so many different voices out here, armchair critics, real critics – that it's hard to find your own voice. So how did you find your voice as a critic? I think you just really hit on that, but how did you find your voice as a critic?

Kendrick: Yeah. I mean it's sort of an extension of what I

was talking about. I think part of it is that I just sort of stumbled into it. I had experience, like I was joking with you earlier, I wrote film reviews in high school but those were certainly more armchair critic reviews. They were like, "Oh, this actor is really great in this movie." Or something that was just objectively "This person acted well enough that you didn't notice they were bad" or something. But as I really began to take this a little bit more seriously, I think a lot of it was just really relying on what I was most interested in saying about a movie and having confidence in that.

So there are people that I follow and really respect and really love that really do dig into that technical aspect of the filmmaking process or maybe they even have a more holistic thing. They have interesting things to say about the story, but they also have interesting things to say about the texture of the film or something. But for me, it was more like "I know what I brought to the table", which is this understanding of storytelling and character. And whether or not someone is really in command of their character and their story such that by the end of the movie, you can say, "OK, that's a complete package, like this person understood what they were trying to accomplish from A to B."

I really didn't bog myself down too much in talking about things that I knew other people could talk about more intelligently. I just really leaned into what I thought I brought to the table. And I would touch on those other things but the meat of my reviews – even the structure of them, really– I usually set them up by saying mini blurb for someone who's never known what The Avengers were or have never heard of Elizabeth Olsen when she was in Martha Marcy May Marlene or something. So I would set it up a little bit just because we did try – at least with

Screen Rant – to be a bit more of a bridge between casual and cinephiles.

So I would do that, and then I would almost immediately talk about whether or not the story worked and whether or not the characters worked. Most of the things that came towards the end of my reviews as I sort of spun out into other areas – like if it's an action movie, if they had special effects or something. And then also trying to contextualize a little bit for people whether or not the movie was good– even if a movie was bad, whether or not people might still enjoy it, if they were looking for a certain type of experience. I might say the story doesn't work but if the action was awesome and it was eye-candy and it was all these cool things happening, maybe that's what someone would want from a Transformers movie or something. Maybe the story doesn't matter as much.

That was sort of how I built my voice – to lean really hard into the story and the characters, which is what I cared about the most, and then cover my butt a little bit by touching on the other things. And also being willing to acknowledge the people who maybe aren't as technical when it comes to the writing or the visuals or whatever. They might still enjoy something that we didn't like as a film community –critic community – because of what they wanted out of it.

Kevin: Got it. All right. So if it's true that there are only 7 basic plots in the world, how do you keep a fresh eye for every movie that you see?

Kendrick: Yeah. I tend to gravitate towards movies that do something special with those 7 plots. And I think that is a thing you notice when you see a lot of movies, that every movie is – I mean anytime there is a generalization like that, I'm reluctant to fully embrace it because it does seem diminishing that people bring sincerity and stuff even if they end up telling the same story.

But I think something like Me and Earl and the Dying Girl is a good example of this. There are probably a lot of stories about an adolescent kid dealing with a friend dying of cancer. I don't feel like that's probably the first movie, by any stretch, or certainly not the first book or the first anything that has ever dealt with that subject matter. But the movie itself had enough – I use the word texture a lot – but it had enough texture and weather around it that made it feel unique, sincere and genuine.

So even if it's a story where I kind of knew how it was going to end – just because movies like that tend to end a certain way – I was still taken with individual moments that grounded this story and these characters as their own thing. As real as fictional people can be – even if the story itself is a story that's pointed in a direction that people have maybe travelled before. I remember specifically in that movie – in one of the last scenes he goes into her room and she's gone, but he discovers she has this hobby that I'd never seen before that he didn't know that she did.

She could create these really beautiful carvings inside of books. She would carve out the pages of the books and make shapes and she chronicled some of her journey that way. And it was this really breathtaking moment in a movie where we were all as an audience – with the character – discovering this hidden talent that you never even knew this person had that was so beautiful and so poetic.

So I think it's a lot like if someone is going to show up and they're like, "You know what? The Transformers movie did really well so I'm going to do a movie about big giant robots and these robots aren't from outer space or whatever. We made them and now they are fighting on earth." You see through that kind of thing.

If you see a movie where someone has a specific intention and feeling and message that they're trying to communicate to people, and it's coming from a place of sincerity or inspiration – I don't think every action movie that's ever come out is coming from a sincere, poetic place, necessarily. But it might be coming from a place where they have a new technology, like new CGI technology that they are excited about. Avatar is a good example of that, right?

I mean Avatar was basically FernGully, which was a rip on a bunch of other colonial stories. We saw Avatar and were blown away by it because the story wasn't what mattered the most in that movie. It was transporting you through this new technology and to this subversive world. That's partially why that movie doesn't hold up to a lot of people long term, because it was a version of a story that had been told. But we were all enamored with it at the time.

Kevin: Right. Okay. Only three more questions. What advice do you have for the up-and-coming critic or a movie reviewer?

Kendrick: Yeah, for sure. The advice that I always give people – and I think I have lived this advice and I've also paid it forward – is that the main thing is just to write. It's to write or record podcasts or do YouTube videos or Twitch stream or whatever. Whatever format you're most interested in being a film critic, just do a lot of that, get better at it and take real feedback. Be realistic about it too, because I feel like there are a lot of people in the industry now that didn't work for it or they think the fact they've done a lot of it means that they are entitled to be successful in it. And that's not really how it works!

The people that I've seen really excel are the people that wrote a lot or whatever medium they were working in – they did a lot of that. And then people gave them feedback and they took that feedback and were really sincere about it. Maybe they didn't take all of the feedback because they disagreed with [parts of] it and people were watering them down, but they made a conscious decision.

I tend to think there are a lot of people that think that they're special and they feel like it should be handed to them. I've always felt very lucky and very fortunate for being able to do what I do. A lot of it came with a lot of hard work, relationships that suffered and a lot of bad stuff because of how hard I was working at it. But I can say throughout that process I really was gleaning feedback and there were times where I would get feedback and I'd be like, "Oh yeah. You know what? I do do that a lot and maybe I should work on that element of my perspective and I should try and open my mind a little bit." Or, "You know what? There's a lot of people saying that I'm not as good at this but I'm great at this so maybe I should lean into this other thing even though I saw myself doing it this way".

So, I think it's a balance between trying to be receptive to that feedback and then also staying true to yourself. But I see a lot of people burn out in the industry because they think they have it and they are already there. I feel like I'm always still learning. I'm still trying to kind of perfect what I'm doing and be more useful in the community and challenge myself in different ways.

The other thing is to get your work out there. People even in this industry have given bad advice and they said "Never write for free" or "Never give your content away for free." I think that comes from a place where there were a lot of publishers and video outlets that were taking advantage of people. I won't name names but I know that there are a lot of user-generated websites that have big names where you can submit your work but you're not going to get paid for it – at all.

And I understand the impulse to rebel against that and say, "Don't let these people take advantage of you." But it also puts a real damper on small websites that you could maybe get in at the ground level. Maybe they don't have enough money to pay you, but you're there and you're hustling and you're gaining experience. You're building a portfolio and you're getting your work set up. Then you're able to take that work and apply to a place like Screen Rant that will pay you and will give you an opportunity. Or that little know-nothing thing that could barely pay you or couldn't pay you at all could be the site that is competing with Screen Rant in three years.

That's what Screen Rant was at one point – it was started by a dude in his basement that knew nothing about film, nothing about writing, and wasn't a particularly good writer. He basically got lucky and also had some skill with SEO so he could get his articles to rank, but then he hired people like me that knew writing and stuff like that and could then take it and run with it.

I feel like some people – and it kind of goes with my last point – do themselves a disservice if you say, "Well, I deserved to be paid" or "I am as good as I need to be in order to be where I want to go." For me, it was a 10-year journey to get where I am. And there were outlets along the way that didn't pay me. There were times where Screen Rant wasn't doing as well as other times and I had to adjust to that.

I don't want to tell anybody, "Don't get paid" or "Don't value what you're worth," because I think that is also an important part of it. However, I don't think there's any shame in hustling for a while and building your portfolio and learning from people that you think have valuable insight – even if they can't roll out the big bucks for you. If you're gaining experience and you're getting better at your craft, eventually you will end up where you want to be if you keep at it.

Kevin: Yeah, I think that's great advice. So the next question is: why is the film critic important?

Kendrick: All right. A question I often struggle with. [Laughter] I think film criticism is kind of like a pejorative in the film industry these days, because critics and the people who ultimately make a film successful or not, often disagree. It used to be that a lot of people will go see a movie, it will make a lot of money because it is fun and it's escapism entertainment or something like that.

I don't think it's wrong that bad movies sometimes do well, and that's what I was sort of talking about earlier. I try to cover my bases a little bit by saying that I can understand why someone likes a Transformers movie. I keep going back to Transformers, which is funny because I actually like those movies more than most critics do – but I understand why they are wildly popular and I understand why critics don't like them. I think the value of a critic's advice is sort of a multifaceted thing.

For one thing, it does push films, directors, and producers to be better, right? If Transformers I comes out and does really well at the box office and it gets average reviews, and then

Transformers II comes out and it gets panned by critics and maybe it makes as much money at the box office – at some level, film producers and directors know that they can't just keep delivering bad movies. So, I do think film critics hold filmmakers and studios accountable a little bit, maybe more than the public does. The public does that sort of through their wallet but that tends to be after they've been fooled into seeing movies that are less than satisfying a couple times. I feel like film critics are sometimes able to verbalize also what people don't like about a movie even if they [the people] don't really know how to verbalize it.

It's also important, in any art form, that there are people that are trying to look at it on a deeper level. It's the same for photography. It's the same for sculpture. It's the same for – even sports and things like that. You want people out there who are digging deeper into something than the people who are watching someone playing basketball. You're still interested in hearing what someone who's a basketball expert and has spent years studying the best basketball players in the world – has to say about this [particular] basketball player, right?

I think it's kind of a two-fold thing at the point at which people say, "Well, no one listens to film critics so it's not useful anymore." That's kind of a bummer because that means people aren't going to be looking as deep into the films, and some films aren't made to be looked into as deeply as others. But I certainly want to read reviews of Me and Earl and the Dying Girl from film critics, not just people who said, "I like this" or "I didn't [like this]." I want to understand what someone sees in that movie at a deeper level. I want people digging into it and gaining a better appreciation for it. Especially if later I see that movie and it really connects with me, and I don't know why it connected with me as much. Having those reviews out there and being able to see why other people connected to it I think is really valuable.

There are certainly ways that – while people may not listen to Rotten Tomatoes and stuff – and I'm not a huge fan of aggregates that take all of the reviews and punch out a number. I mean for sure a rotten review or score on Rotten Tomatoes can dramatically impact the box office of a film. So, having as many qualified voices with interesting takes and getting as many voices in the room so that it isn't just a group of people shutting down a movie that they may not really have connected with – I think there's a value to that too and kind of even in a commercial way.

Kevin: Yeah. Most definitely. I wish I could talk back on this, but I'm just getting all your answers. [Laughter]

Kendrick: Yup. Yup.

Kevin: All right. Last question is: where do you see film criticism headed?

Kendrick: Yeah. I mean it's kind of fake news, right? I'm curious to see where online journalism in general goes from here, because now there is sort of a culture of people shouting down voices that they disagree with as being illegitimate or as untrue or inherently valueless or something like that. And it's kind of weird because that's not really how – especially film criticism or any form of criticism – has ever worked. There's certainly people whose voices should probably be louder than others but if I have a friend who likes movies and he is an armchair film critic, his opinion has value.

So the idea to say that no one should be able to tell me what

I think or what they think of a film to influence my opinion, is kind of ridiculous to me. Like I said, it's sort of the same thing with fake news – if you disagree with me, you just say, "Oh well, that's fake news." Or you're like, "You're just saying that because Disney is paying you to give a positive review of Avengers." But you're undercutting someone's opinion as being disingenuous for the purpose of furthering their political agenda or that you're getting some monetary benefits that no one knows about or something like that.

It's going to be interesting because film criticism falls into that same category that there inherently is going to be a skepticism towards people who you disagree with. You would think something like Rotten Tomatoes where you had to be verified as a real film critic in one way or another would have been the litmus test for that. That's not proving to be the case. It's proving to be that, if anything, that may have muddied the water some. I feel like it's always going to be a thing that is there because people are always going to want to talk about these movies.

But, I feel like it may already be happening that there are two versions of this, which is this kind of armchair film criticism – and maybe that becomes more accepting, like people may just say, "Listen, I don't listen to critics. I'm more interested in what people like me have to say about this film."

And so, that ends up being where those people get their information from. Then there are still people that want to read dyed-in-the-wool film critics and those people are going to be there too. It just may be that the film critic, this person that's put on a pedestal – or slapped down by people who disagree with them – has less weight because people are just going to pick and choose the kind of feedback on a film they want.

One of the big takeaways for me, which is why I suggest people read film reviews now – maybe this is kind of what will happen to it. And this would be the ideal scenario as far as I'm concerned. I don't like it if people look at Rotten Tomatoes and make a judgment on a film based solely on the critical consensus.

I think the real value of Rotten Tomatoes is that it exposes you to thousands of critical perspectives and each of those people has a profile on there that you can bookmark, or you can save their feed or whatever. You can say, "You know what? This Ben Kendrick guy, he is full of it. I can't stand his perspective on this stuff. I don't like him. I don't like anything about him. But Rob Key, any time Rob Key posts a review, I tend to agree with the kinds of films he likes. I love the way he talks about film."

If you bookmark Rob's Rotten Tomatoes and every time he posts about a film you want to see and you read his takes before you go see it, that's the ideal scenario. Maybe it's a little bit of an echo chamber, like you may not be challenged as much or something. At least then you're reading a thought-out film review as opposed to just going and talking to your friends or something. It's interesting.

I'm kind of curious if culturally we eventually will have a sort of renaissance where this kind of stuff – people become interested in this stuff again and they're less dismissive of opinions that are different from theirs. But it seems like we're still in the early days of the internet – which is sort of horrifying to think about, but maybe we'll pull ourselves back. Right now, we're in kind of a growth place but yeah, that's my take.

I don't know. I think local voices are kind of gone, which is sort of a bummer. Like Lisa Kennedy, the film critic in Denver, and I think Robert Denerstein [The Rocky Mountain News]. They were the local film critics in Denver. I remember I read their film reviews every week before I would go see movies. I didn't always listen to them, but they were the Denver film critics and both of those people lost their jobs a decade ago, almost. I think the Rocky Mountain News is gone – and I think the Rocky Mountain News basically syndicates reviews from Rolling Stone or something now. I don't think they have their own dedicated film critics.

So it certainly seems like it's moving towards a broad online thing that has less to do with your local paper. That's why I think picking out the reviewers you dig on Rotten Tomatoes is sort of the ideal scenario right now, at least.

CHAPTER 10

EMMA LOGGINS

Name: Emma Loggins

Medium: Online

Outlet: Fanbolt

Years active: 18

Top 3 movies: Jurassic Park, Lord of The Rings, Amelie

Favorite Director: Steven Spielberg

Emma Loggins is the Editor in Chief of FanBolt. As an internationally recognized "Geek Girl", Emma creates daily updates on the latest entertainment news, her opinions on current happenings in the media, various screening/filming opportunities, inside scoops and more. She's been writing on the world of geekdom and pop culture since 2002 and is also considered to be one of the top Atlanta bloggers and influencers!

Emma is a boss, both literally and that hashtag-cool type! She was super transparent with me, sharing how she got into film criticism as a way to escape the harsh reality of life as a high school nerd. If you're reading this book, it's likely because movies mean the world to you. Emma is an example of how you can channel a negative into a positive with that love for film (and television). Her story is inspirational! She's a fighter and a much needed voice in the field!

Kevin: All right, Emma. When did you first fall in love with film?

Loggins: It's so hard for me to pinpoint the exact moment that that happened. I would jokingly probably say it was the same moment I realized I had my first crush on Harrison Ford for Indiana Jones. But I really grew up with film being such a huge part of my life. As a kid, I was really obsessed with Disney movies. For me, the highlight of my summer vacation would be finishing school with a soundtrack that just came out on cassette in May for the film that was coming out in June. I'd listen to it on my Walkman on repeat until the film would come out and it was just the best moment of the summer for me.

But I was obsessed with so many films. Indiana Jones, ET, The Goonies, I just – all of the '80s for me were like VHS tapes and watching movies on HBO or Showtime. And it just really made my childhood. I didn't really see film as something separate. It was just a part of me and my life and just allowed for me to escape into this magical world and experience the story as if I was a character in it.

I think being exposed to film at such an early age is really a large part of where my creativity came from and the need to be creative, and a creative was really born in me. So I was making radio shows on my cassette recorder and making movies on our giant camcorder when I was like 5. I just – it was always such a huge part of my life.

Kevin: Awesome. What drew you to the art of film criticism? And specifically, obviously with your blog, it's more of an editorial. I think that there is this line where we go from being kids that just love it to actually wanting to speak about films in a critical way. So, what drew you to the

art of film criticism?

Loggins: Well, for me, I kind of had your stereotypical high school experience. I was a nerd who was obsessed with my grades and I got bullied a lot. So I didn't have a lot of friends. I kind of hated that whole part of my life. So, I found escape through film and television and they brought these worlds where I could escape and live another life and have a break from harassment or the realization that my life wasn't what I wanted it to be at that moment.

So I was very protective of the movies and the shows that I loved. And I think my need to protect what I love is kind of what first drew me to reviewing. I would review episodes of TV shows I loved and analyze what a character said or did or the music that was picked. I would even record movies from HBO or my favorite shows on VHS and I would make cases for them; I think that's probably where my love for graphic design stemmed from initially.

But later when DVDs became introduced and I started doing DVD reviews, I would rip apart music choices that replaced the original music choices on the show because when they originally air they didn't buy the music rights for the home release and that really bothered me because it wasn't the same experience. So I think I started getting more upset over things with that experience and it not being the beautiful form of whatever it was that I originally enjoyed.

The more and more I found myself going down that path, I just became more opinionated. I never really considered myself a film critic. I was just a film lover. I love talking about them and it's what my reviews were and I still feel like that holds true for me. Only now, I really love reviewing bad movies too because those are actually, I think, the most fun to review and kind of tear into.

But I think it was really that whole process of just reviewing episodes of TV shows that kind of introduced me into reviewing things and then ultimately that led into reviewing films and DVD reviews and then film reviews.

Kevin: Perfect. Next question is how did you find your voice as a critic? Because I think for me when I was first trying to get into film criticism, I couldn't track down a mentor and nobody wanted to talk to me. And then on top of that, we have so many voices now and anybody can kind of be a critic. So it's really tough to kind of stick to your guns and find your own voice. So how did you do that?

Loggins: Yeah. I think it's – I almost want to say it's probably more challenging now than it was when I got into it. For me, it was just a one way conversation. It was like a long-winded answer to a question a friend would ask, did you like this movie? Why or why not?

For me, I think that then became a formula on my site for my reviews. They followed the same formula. The first paragraph would answer the question of what the movie was about, then the second paragraph would be how the cast performed, and then the next would be the technical elements in the film. I'd talk about the special effects quality or the cinematography that was – if it was worth noting, how the film soundtrack was. Then I would go into any issues that I had with the film and close with my kind of summarizing thoughts about what I felt about the film overall. And it was a formula that helps me kind of keep it short and sweet but also deliver my opinion in a way that felt honest and organized. I've always branded myself as a geek girl.

I love geeking out over things whether that's film, television, food, travel, anything that I'm really passionate about. And with film being one of those main things that I geek out over, I want my passion and my love for film to come through on my reviews. I think by kind of doing it that way, I was able to come at everything from a positive place.

I remember when I first heard reviewing films, I was actually kind of scared to do a negative review because I was building these relationships with studios and I was worried that if I give a bad review to something that would burn my bridges with studios. So I remember this little trick I did in the beginning where I would explain something and then I would say, "Well, if you like these types of movies then you'll love this movie," to kind of make it – like still being true to what I felt about it but then kind of trying to make it a nicer way of saying that the movie wasn't good by comparing it to other movies that I didn't think were good.

But the more I did it and the more I kind of felt like my voice was established in that space, I was able to just get real with it and not really care about the blow back of whether or not studios or readers agreed with what I had to say.

Kevin: All right. So I'm going to camp out on this really quickly because I think what you just brought up is very important and it's something that all critics kind of struggle with, and that's with the negative review. So I like what you said in that you just got to a point where, "Hey, I don't care. I'm just going to speak the truth,". Which I think at the end of the day, it's that authenticity that people gravitate towards. But I've literally seen critics who come out of a screening at a festival and they will say nice things to the

director while they're walking through the hall but then be like, "That movie sucked." [Chuckle]

Loggins: Right.

Kevin: But this is a real thing, right? So like you don't want to burn bridges kind of as you said but at the same time like I think authenticity and the authentic voice is everything. So the question is how did you get over that hurdle of going from that point of trying to protect yourself, your brand, to "I know my brand is going to be honest and that's just a part of it"?

Loggins: Right. Right. I mean it's – I think it was something that the further I kind of got into it, I was dealing with this PR company that would represent these movies that came into town. I'd get early screening passes and I would go, come out of the theater, give my initial reactions and then I would email them in my film review after embargo was up.

After doing that for a year or two, even the same with the DVD reviews, it was never directly – I think all the other ones were through a PR company that was kind of like middlemen. It kind of gave me this false sense of security that if I was going to say something negative, I'm not saying it directly to the studio. However, the more I did it, I realized, you know, it doesn't really matter. Studios have tons of films that are coming out. PR companies are representing tons of films. They know something is not good just as much as you know something is not good. It's not a secret. So I feel like the honesty is so important not only to your own integrity but also, the way studios, PR companies and everyone else views what you write. If you're writing something that's always continuously nice and complimentary then it's going to be obvious that you a) don't know what you're talking about, or b) you have a bad taste in film.

So being honest is so, so important and just realizing at the end of the day that if you rip into a movie and give it a horrific review– no one is going to lose a job over it. The movie is already made. The people that are going to go see it are going to go see it anyways. It's not going to be something that makes or breaks the studio or a film.

That being said, I still haven't mastered the art of directly telling like a film director, "I don't like your movie." I think that's more personal and it's something where in a lot of cases they have poured their heart and their soul into making something and it just wasn't a good outcome. They probably know that deep down but they don't want that salt rubbed in their wound when you're coming out of a festival [screening].

So I'll either usually avoid those interactions or I'll just say, "Congratulations on having your film selected to play here. That's going to be such a cool thing for you." And I just kind of avoid being like, "Yeah, that really wasn't good. You did a horrible job on this movie."

So those were kind of my techniques. But really, I think it's – so much of it is just getting comfortable in this industry and realizing that your voice is one of hundreds if not thousands of critics that are talking about this film and what you say isn't going to make or break it. So just be honest and be true to yourself and that's what's going to help you build your credibility and your readership in this space.

Kevin: Nice. And I love what you said in terms of remembering the studio knows when they've got a dud on their hands.

Loggins: Yeah.

Kevin: Because we know so many times like there's a cold open or there's this mad rush at the last second where the stars are actually coming on your podcast or something.

[Laughter]

Loggins: Right.

Kevin: Just like wait a second, this never happens.

[Laughter]

Loggins: Exactly.

Kevin: All right. So let's go to the next question. If it's true there are only 7 basic plots in the world, how do you keep a fresh eye for every movie or TV show that you see?

Loggins: Well, I feel like that it's such a sad way to look at it even if it is true. I don't feel like that's something that I as a film lover would point out. I think if you break things down into such a science like that, you look at it differently. If you're looking at something as a science, I feel like it's hard to really appreciate the creative nature of something.

For me when I sit down and I watch a movie, I'm going into 90 minutes or however long of story time. Someone is telling me a story that they've created and I'm trying as hard as possible to submerge myself in that world that they're creating. I'm trying to relate to a character and see myself in that position and really just submerge myself in it.

Now, if I can't do that, then the plot issues or the acting or the script problems or whatever all become really apparent to me and I start picking it apart while I'm watching it. But for me, I'm going into every movie I see as a film lover with a clean slate. I want to enjoy it. I want to break out from my daily routine to experience a new life view or a new culture or a new world that I otherwise wouldn't be able to experience.

So I feel like coming at it from that angle allows me to keep a fresh eye for every movie I see. I never go searching for reviews for something or opinions about something before I see it. Now, sometimes I will stumble into that or someone I'm sitting next to at a screening will say, "Oh, this isn't getting good buzz or something like that." That can sometimes taint my view on it.

But – and if it's something like that where I hear that, I'm going in with even lower expectations. So I'm even more likely to probably like it more than I would have just because my expectations have been lowered. But I try to really just keep it a clean slate for myself and go in not knowing what other people's opinions are and really just trying to submerge myself into the story.

Kevin: Awesome. What advice do you have for the up-and-coming critic?

Loggins: I would say, just start writing. I have a lot of kids that email me that are in high school and they're looking for some sort of – I actually just had one that had emailed me for a senior project that they were working on and needed a mentor for the project to sign off on stuff for school, which is cool because that totally wasn't a thing back in the early 2000s when I did it. It was just you're on your own. Figure it out.

But I would say, write for your school newspaper or start a blog. Just start posting your reviews on social media or a message board or something. The best way to start something is just to start it. You never really know what you can really build until you start building it. And if you want to make being a film critic something that you actually are paid for, the more experience you have, the more desirable you'll obviously be when you apply for those jobs.

I tell high school kids all the time, "Send me writing samples and if I can feel your love and your passion for film in your writing then I'll totally bring you on as a volunteer writer for the site." And I feel like a lot of sites would probably do that as well. We're all looking for good content. It never hurts to reach out and ask. It's just a good way for them to start getting their name out there and grow their skills and add something to their resume.

Kevin: Why is the film critic important? I guess on the flip-side you could say, is the film critic important?

[Laughter]

Loggins: I do think it's important. I think it's important because I think films are important. You can't really evaluate art without criticism. Good art makes you feel something whether it's something good or something bad. I would argue if you don't feel anything at all then that's bad art.

You can't truly appreciate something if you don't look at all the pieces that make it up. You lose sight of the real meaning or the cultural importance that films offer if you don't fully examine and analyze them. No matter how great a film is or how horrible it is in your opinion, each one is a piece of art. Someone has a story, a thought, or an idea that they are trying to express in every movie they make and the way in which they do that is art to me.

So even more I'd argue that some of the most amazing Indie films are documentaries. We'd get lost without film critics highlighting how amazing they are and the industry would only have room for the big blockbusters then. So I think the film critics give smaller films a chance to be seen and appreciated just as much as the bigger films which I think it's really important.

Kevin: Perfect. All right. Last question. Where do you see film criticism headed?

Loggins: That's a hard one to predict because I feel like when I started doing this, it was before Facebook and MySpace was even a thing and it's kind of crazy how social media has changed so much of this. But I feel like our attention spans are definitely getting shorter and shorter and people are getting busier and busier in their daily lives. I think we're probably going to see reviews going more short form than a lot of the longer form reviews we've seen.

I have this app on my phone that basically chops nonfiction books up into like 15-minute doses where they can convey all of the takeaways from a book within 15 minutes and you can walk out with the same knowledge of if you had spent several hours reading the book. So many of us are kind of looking for that ways to be more efficient and spend less time on things, and so much of digital media is headed that way.

You hear that videos that you're uploading to YouTube need to be no longer than 3 minutes but really no longer than a minute and a half. You start losing people when they see that there's a real time investment. And I think if you go to a page where you're scrolling down and it's really long, it's intimidating, which is sad. It's really sad but it's the reality of the world we live in today. So I think if I had to make a prediction about where it's headed, I would say that we're going to see more of an increase in short form reviews and not as many long form reviews.

CHAPTER 11

KEVIN MCCARTHY

Name: Kevin McCarthy

Medium: Radio, Television

Outlet: Fox 5 DC, 106.7 The Fan

Years active: 13

Top 3 movies: Terminator 2: Judgement Day, True Romance, Jaws

Favorite Director: Alfred Hitchcock and Quentin Tarantino

Kevin McCarthy has been a film critic in the Washington DC metro area since 2005, where he is also currently a member of the Washington Area Film Critics Association and Critics Choice Association. You can find his reviews on CBS RADIO and the Local DC FOX affiliate. He graduated from George Mason University in the spring of 2006 and majored in Communications with a concentration in media production and criticism.

Kevin began his movie reviewing career on The Junkies, a morning show, heard on 106.7 WJFK-FM (CBS RADIO), along with hosting his own weekly movie show on Friday evenings. In the summer of 2007, Kevin was hired as the movie reviewer for the Fox 5 morning news. He became known for his conversational writing style and unique rating system. Kevin appears on The Junkies every Friday morning and will continue to make appearances on FOX 5 TV. His favorite film of all time is "True Romance" and he considers "The Godfather Part 2" to be the greatest film ever made.

There's no doubt that Kevin's love for film is palpable! He bleeds cinema. Sometimes, watching, reading, or listening to another critic's work can help inform your own. With Kevin, I learned the power of constructing key questions for interviews. If you've ever watched one of his interviews, you know a few things: he's done his homework on his subject, he knows their body of work, he understands filmmaking and he combines it all to create unique, memorable questions that make him a favorite amongst those he interviews. How does he do it? Keep reading.

Kevin: When did you first fall in love with film?

McCarthy: I was eight years old. Terminator 2: Judgment Day was coming out in theaters and my parents wouldn't let me see it because it was Rated R. I remember them going out to see it without me and I was very upset. I think we had a babysitter, her name was Tiffany, and she stayed home with my brother and I. I remember being super upset because of the commercials for Terminator 2, if I remember them correctly, it was just the visual effects. And at that time I didn't know who James Cameron was or anything like that. But Arnold Schwarzenegger became my favorite actor professionally my entire life – when I was a little kid because of that movie.

But yeah, Terminator 2 basically, it – so they went and saw it, they got back. I think it was the same night they got back that I came up with a plan and I told them if I get a good report card, could we rent the film on VHS when it comes to Blockbuster or whatever. I remember like my report card at that time S's as in Sam, N as in Nancy and U. So Satisfactory, Needs Improvement and Unsatisfactory were the ratings you got. And I was getting some Ns at that point. I don't remember if I had any Us but I was always that kid in class who kind of raises his hand and asks a lot of questions. I think teachers thought I was ADD and things like that but I was just that guy in class that asks a lot of questions. It turns out I actually am ADD but that was a –

[laughter]

McCarthy: But yeah, so – I told my parents if I get a perfect report card can I watch Terminator 2 with you guys? The movie, I don't remember, I don't think the movie has any like sex or nudity in it so it was just the violence and the language are kind of the things that were problematic. I ended up working really hard. I got all S's. I think it was my third grade report card. Then we rented the film on VHS, it was just a month or two months after release date and I sat there and watched it.

I remember just falling in love with filmmaking at that point. I'm just digging in to how movies are made and the magic trick in it all. And how Cameron pulled off the special effects, specifically the T-1000 effects, and Robert Patrick coming out of the ground, that coffee sequence, and just everything. I mean everything about the visual effects and Arnold and just everything that Stan Winston did back at the – you know I didn't know who Stan Winston was at that time which tied to go over the effects of Arnold's character and the machine and… It was just amazing.

I used to like dream of being Edward Furlong in the sense of being in a movie with Arnold and then Arnold releases film called Last Action Hero – just like the ultimate fanboy moment to have a movie where a guy goes into a movie and acts across from Arnold, that was surreal. So yeah, that was – that was the moment – that was the movie that made me fall in love with film.

Kevin: Awesome. All right. Second question, what drew you to the art of film criticism? Because I think that you know it's one thing to be the kid on the couch, you know you convince your parents, "Hey, I want to watch this film." but then over the years to be like – you know I actually want to drill my voice in the ring on what these films actually means. So, what drew you to the art of film criticism?

McCarthy: Yeah, I mean it's interesting. I never really kind of envisioned myself as being a critic, either on television or radio. I'm not really a TV person or a radio person. I think the weird thing about my job specifically over the years is that I've just kind of been myself with regards to talking to people. I talk to my friends the way I talk on the air about movies.

So, I always just love speaking about movies and you know obviously I watched Siskel and Ebert growing up. When I was a kid my dad would get the New York Times and I would love opening up the Times and see that the full page Sunday ads for the films that were coming out. I'd see the review quotes on the there [thinking] like "that's cool job, how cool is that to to talk about movies and have people like listen to you about it?."

When I was in college I was a Media Criticism and Production major so I was actually more into the production side. I was heavily into editing, cinematography – if you listen to my interviews when I was on radio, it was just really kind of behind the scene stuff with composers and cinematographers. So I just always found talking about the inner works of movies to be fascinating. My favorite thing was watching the DVD and Blu-ray features and then explain to people how directors shot these things.

I remember when Dark Knight came out (I was so obsessed with Chris Nolan) and the behind the scenes featurette about Dark Knight. I loved to tell people about how they did certain scenes. So, I always found a lot of joy in talking to people about film and just how movies were done. There's a movie opening this weekend called Tag and then and like there's the whole situation in that film is Renner in real life broke his arm and that his arms were basically CGI throughout the film. So, I always get a kick out of talking to people about those things.

I want to make the person you see in the movie experience it kind of as exciting as I do. So, if somebody is in a theater watching a movie and they heard something I mentioned in the review and it enhances their experience, that's kind of – that makes me so happy. If someone tweets me and says, "Hey man, I saw these things mentioned in the review…" and not to make it about me but just to give themselves some more insight into enjoying the theater experience.

Also, I'm a big advocate of theaters, movie cinema and sending people to a theater to see a movie in the best possible way. And over the years as I've been a critic, I try to embrace the different formats that studios are putting movies out in: 3D, IMAX, things like that. I'm trying to steer people in the right direction as to how to spend their money, you know, makes sure you see Dunkirk in 70 millimeter IMAX or things like that. There are just ways to watch films that I think that people need to be educated on in regards to when they go to a box office with 15 different reasons.

But to answer your question specifically, yeah, I was always more a fan of the production side, the critic part of it kind of came from me speaking to my friends a certain way about movies. Then going on a radio show to talk about films and just that passion of like – of talking to people about the inner workings of how a movie is made and hopefully, hopefully enhancing someone's experience. But initially I want to be a lawyer, just you know, weirdly enough, I wanted to be a lawyer when I was in high school. And then…

Kevin: What?

McCarthy: Yeah. I was – and then I found out there was so much reading involved. I was like, "Nope, I'm not doing that."

[Laughter]

McCarthy: So I got out of that mindset. The movies were always my first love, but I didn't think I'd ever have a place in this business. And then the production side of things kind of enhanced my viewing of how I view films, and enhanced my passion of explaining to people how movies are made and that's kind of how the critic element came into play.

Kevin: All right. Got you. So, kind of piggybacking off of that and I love what you said just in terms of you've always been yourself. The fact that you're a fan of the production, it really comes through. And so that leads into the next question which is how did you find your voice as a critic?

Because for me, personally, even you know, critic to critic, I've learned so much from you in terms of like how you put together a question. I think you do a phenomenal job of ensuring the interview is not just straight stale, the same old, same old when these actors or directors are running the press circuit. But how did you find your voice as a critic specifically to not be like anyone else but just be you?

McCarthy: Yeah, well, thank you for saying that. It's interesting, I don't remember when I cut the switch off in my mind about just be yourself. I guess when you get into television and radio, there's this mindset that you need to speak a certain way or look a certain way or talk a certain way. I always found people latched on to genuine passion. So when it comes to finding my voice there was a moment, I can't remember specifically when it happened, when I realized "just go into these interview rooms and just be you and just ask questions."

So, a buddy of mine, his name is Jake, he works in Chicago. I remember he told me something really early on when we first met back in 2010. He said "ask questions that you just genuinely want to know the answer to." I remember that stuck with me because if I go in a room and I'm talking to an actor and I want to know something genuinely, they feed off that and then they get excited about it as well. Especially with audiences watching my reviews or things like that. People sometimes tell me they don't even go to the movie but they like watching my segments because it's just somebody who's genuinely passionate about what they're doing. So, I think people latch on to passion and I think if you're genuine about what you're doing, people will react in a positive way.

It's kind of more along the lines of sitting across from someone, like a Steven Spielberg or somebody, which is kind of surreal to even way out loud, if you ask him things that you want to know the answers to, he'll open up about it. I think there's the delivery thing, the way you ask it. I mean I get nervous with every interview, every segment I do in regards to movie reviewing but there is a – I don't know it's weird. There was a moment I guess I just realized I just need to be me.

The thing about my type of criticism is I really heavily focus on the behind the scenes stuff. So, I have a hard time balancing how some people just want to know, is the movie good? I don't really like that question because it's yes or no and I feel like there's a lot more to a movie review than is the movie good or not? I find that there are so many things that you can find that was in the film that you like or dislike and I try to cover that within the two or three minutes I have to review that movie.

So something clicked and just said be you and just talk to the actors as if you're talking to a friend but also just ask them things you want to ask and tell people on the air about things that you care about in that particular film. You know, if I'm reviewing a Scorsese movie or Spielberg movie, I like to speak on the score, the soundtrack, the music and things like that.

I know what I like about the movie so I express what I like about it to the audience and hopefully they agree or disagree. Sometimes if people don't agree with me they'll go against what I say. So, for example, if I loved a movie they won't see it, if I hate it they will see it. Which is cool because they're still utilizing the review.

Kevin: Right, right. All right. If it's true that there are only seven basic plot points or plots in the world, how do you keep a fresh eye for every movie you see?

McCarthy: Well, it's interesting because every movie we see is – I mean obviously, you and I weren't alive when the first movie came out so it's more of a – everything nowadays has been back in the day as well. Every filmmaker learns from other filmmakers. So, someone like Spielberg or Quentin Tarantino was just a kid watching movies in a movie theatre and they made movies based on what they like.

So, I think that the structure of a story is going to be mostly similar in filmmaking. But I think it's the – and Ron Howard actually said this in his master class recently about bringing a fresh take to a familiar storyline. Every movie generally fills a certain structure of beginning, middle and end. Hereditary for example, I've never seen anything like Hereditary but we've seen movies that are like that. We've seen movies about spiritual elements, demonic possessions and things like that, but it was done in a different way.

So, I think the beauty of film is it's almost nearly impossible to find something truly original but you can. I was watching Get Out recently and I was watching Jordan Peele's commentary. Everything in the commentary was him referencing other films like "I did this shot because of this shot. I did this shot because of this shot in this movie." Chris Nolan sat down at theatre and watched 2001 for the first time in like 1977 or whatever it was. Now all of that is coming through his movies.

So like Dunkirk and Interstellar and Inception are extremely, heavily Kubrick influenced. I think it's just a matter of taking what you've learned through watching movies, in my opinion, and putting your own fresh take and spin on it. I think that that's point. Tarantino is like the biggest movie fan on the planet and everything he does is directly related to films he loved. I mean I think he'll probably walk you through one of his movies and every moment is probably a reference or an homage or something. So, to me, it's putting your own spin on something already love. So it's almost impossible to find something truly original. It's just going to be the way you put your spin on it.

Kevin: What advice do you have for the up and coming critic?

McCarthy: My particular story and advice is based on the quote I heard from a radio professor of mine at George Mason which is "do what you love and the money will follow." I mean I did this job that I'm doing now practically, almost for free, for about eight years. I got hired at Fox full-time in 2013 but I was working a sales assistant job at CBS for the first eight years. I started sort of making a little bit of money in between that but it wasn't a lot. But I never did this job for money. I never even went into this job looking for any money.

And you know I probably shouldn't say this but I would do what I'm doing now for free, no question. I mean it's just one of those things where I just genuinely love what I do. The way that I looked at it was looking at it like I'm having four minutes with Steven Spielberg I mean – I'll pay someone to be there. You know what I mean?

So I think if you want it enough, I think you'll make it happen. Just don't go into it for the money because the money may take a while. And it might not be a ton of money. You know what I mean? So, it's one of those things where, in my opinion, if you love something enough just do it. But I mean then again, there is a balance of not being taken advantage of and obviously having to live and eat and you know things like that. So, there is a balance to it and I think that everyone's story is different being a critic nowadays. YouTube is big way to get your reviews out there, social media, etc. Just find things you like in these movies and talk about them. Just keep trying and pushing yourself, but online, really that YouTube element is probably my biggest advice. With popular videos on YouTube you'll never know who's going to find them or see them.

So, yeah, just be you and talk about the things that you love about film and don't worry about what other people think about your reviews just because there are people who agree and disagree with you and I think if you're polarizing then you're doing something right. So, just keep going.

Kevin: Why is the film critic important? And I guess on the flip side of that you could say, is the film critic important?

McCarthy: Oh yeah, 100%. Film criticism is extremely important and movie studios would completely agree with that because when a movie has great reviews that helps the box office. But if it got a bad review, it could hurt the box office clearly. So, I think in regards to the business of movies, movie critics are vey important in regards to getting a voice of a movie out there. However, I think movie reviewing is more important for films that need to be talked about more. When I go on the air and review Avengers: Infinity War, I mean I love that movie, but I think that that kind of movie probably was going to be fine without it. But I will say Infinity War probably did as well as it did because everyone loved it so much.

So, I think that criticism is important – you know putting aside the box office and things like that – it's important because so many people view a movie differently through different eyes, different lenses, different perspectives. Someone might have a different take on 2001: A Space Odyssey than I do and that's awesome. So, I think it's important to have a bunch of different voices speaking on film because it opens up different possibilities for interpretations of those movies. And I think that it's important because you're pointing out things that people might not have looked for while watching a film. You could be enhancing a film for somebody and that's a really big deal.

I think that critics are always going to be very important. I think the problem though, in my opinion, is when critics get a little too negative. What I mean by that is when you're watching a film critically, review a movie how you want. If you hated it, you hated it. If you disliked it, you disliked it. If you loved it, you loved it. But I feel like there's a sense of sometimes people are already negative before walking into a film. Maybe they don't like super hero movies or they don't like whatever. So, I think that the most important thing is to keep an open mind and only do this job if you really love it. I think that if there comes a point that you just don't love reviewing movies anymore, then don't do it, because that's going to come across in your movie reviews and things like that.

So, I think the role of the critic is important if the critic is passionate about what they're doing because it will then translate to people who are watching the film and spread the word about that movie. I just don't like seeing negativity in the critic world in regards to people being critical about movies in general. Reviewing the film itself, that's a totally different story but you should love what you're doing and love the fact that you're reviewing movies!Keep a positive outlook when you walk into a film, and if you don't like it, don't like it, it's totally fine. There's tons of movies that I don't like either but just keep passion in my opinion.

Kevin: Yeah, I can totally relate because as a filmmaker and you obviously made a film as well, so going to school for film, I understand what it takes to actually make it. So, I too agree…

McCarthy: Exactly.

Kevin: …you can say whether you like a film or not but

you have to respect all the time and energy that went into actually creating it. I think sometimes critics will pooh-pooh a film but they couldn't make it themselves. So that's why I'm always like "could you do it?"

McCarthy: Yeah.

Kevin: Last question. Where do you see film criticism headed?

McCarthy: I think that the internet obviously has changed film criticism a lot. Obviously you've heard that line all the time people say "everybody is a critic." And I do think that there needs to be some type I don't know, bar set where – because anybody can upload a movie review to YouTube, anybody can be a particular critic. I just want people who genuinely are working hard as movie critics to be professional critics. But it's hard to say that because I love the idea of somebody being able to upload their reviews to YouTube and then become a critic from that point. You can make money off of your reviews on YouTube.

So, I think it's hard to draw the line as to who is a critic and who isn't but everybody has the right to review a movie and get their thoughts out there. So, I think the internet is changing everything clearly. I mean YouTube, Twitter, Instagram, people are coming up with clever ways to review movies and it's about screenshots now and the thumbnails. I don't know, I just hope that the love of cinema and the idea of what it meant to be a film critic for the longest time still kind of comes through this new technology element as well.

It's very simple for someone who has a camera now to shoot a movie review on their phone. So I hope technology doesn't oversaturate the film critic element. I hope that there's still a core group of trusted critics that people still go to. But then again on the other side of that, I love the idea of someone being able to do their reviews themselves and put them up on YouTube.

So, I think the future of film criticism is going to be more of what we're seeing now. I hope that there is a bar set as to who we're listening to and whose reviews people are watching and things like that. But then again you never know, you can break out on YouTube and become a million subscriber reviewer and then you're a critic. So, it's just one of those things where the technology is kind of shifting the way we view criticism and the way people review movies.

CHAPTER 12

NELL MINOW

Name: Nell Minow

Medium: Online

Outlet: moviemom.com, rogerebert.com, and more

Years active: 23

Top 3 movies: The Philadelphia Story, His Girl Friday, To Have and Have Not

Favorite Director: Preston Sturges, Ernst Lubitsch, Martin Scorsese, George Lucas, Stanley Doman, Steven Spielberg

Nell Minow has been reviewing movies as The Movie Mom since 1995 and appears each week on radio stations across the country to talk about the week's releases in theaters and on DVD/Blu-Ray/streaming. She is Assistant Editor and critic for rogerebert.com and her other reviews appear on this site, along with features, giveaways, interviews, and commentary. She can also be seen on Medium and The Credits. She is a member of the Washington Area Film Critics Association, the Critics Choice Association, the Online Film Critics Association, and the Alliance of Women Film Journalists.

Her articles have appeared in USA Today, Family Fun, Daughters, Parents, and the Chicago Tribune, and she was Yahoo's movie critic for six years. Her books include The Movie Mom's Guide to Family Movies and 101 Must-See

Movie Moments. She has been profiled in the New York Times, the Economist, Forbes, the Chicago Tribune, Working Woman, CFO Magazine, the Ladies Home Journal, Washingtonian Magazine, and the Chicago Sun Times, and has appeared as The Movie Mom on CBS This Morning, Fox Morning News, NPR, CNN, and dozens of radio stations.

When I penned my "Open Letter To Black Screenwriters" back in 2014 (which would lead me to found the DC Black Film Festival), Nell was the first person I asked to read it. If you've ever read one of her think-pieces, or even just her Facebook posts, you know she has a way with words when it comes to making a case for whatever she's advocating. (It could be her work in corporate governance and her family history that plays a role in that, which she discusses below). She helped me cut through some of the unnecessary, personal interjections I had in the letter, to get to the meat and potatoes. Her ability to cut to the heart of a matter and explore the issues is what makes her writing memorable. That's incredibly valuable when you're conveying your thoughts to your audience as a critic.

Kevin: Nell, when did you first fall in love with film?

Minow: Well, according to my dad, I was four years old, I found a letter that he wrote to my grandparents where he said that he had taken me to my first movie, a Disney film called Westward Ho the Wagons! Which I still haven't seen again. He said that after that, every single day I said I wanted to go back to the movies. So apparently, right from the beginning I always loved movies. My parents loved movies, and they still do. I was visiting them this weekend and my dad said, "Please find a good move for us to see." So I showed them Battle of the Sexes.

I grew up in a family also that was very media aware. My

father, when I was nine years old, made a speech to the National Association of Broadcasters. He was President Kennedy's Chairman of the FCC. It was about how television was a vast wasteland and they needed to do a better job. As a result of that, Sherwood Schwartz was so insulted by what my dad said about television that he named the sinking ship on Gilligan's Island after him, the S.S. Minnow. So – [Laughter] so which we –

Kevin: Seriously?

Minow: Oh yeah, 100% serious. So we consider that a compliment, we're very honored by that. So my father was a pioneer in the creation of PBS and cable television. We grew up in a very media attentive house. A house that was very aware of what was good and what was bad, and the importance of being able to tell the difference in media. So, that was a wonderful background for me and I just fell I love with movies right from the beginning.

Kevin: Wow that is a really cool story. So, the next question is what drew you to the art of film criticism?

Minow: You know for me it was really kind of a perfect storm of different experiences and qualities coming together. When I was 16, on the last day of school before summer vacation, so June of my sophomore year, I was diagnosed with a very severe case of mononucleosis. I was confined to bed for the entire summer, and my parents wheeled this tiny little black and white TV into my bedroom since I couldn't leave my bedroom really. So I was pretty much stuck there watching the five channels that were available at the time. There was no DVDs, no VCRs, no cable, no nothing.

So there were five channels and that was such a great

education for me because I would just watch whatever movie was on, which meant (since this was the 1960s) there was a lot of movies from the '40s and '50s. I would never have been exposed to those films really any other way. It gave me a sense, again, of what was good and what was bad, what worked, and what didn't work. It was my beginning to understand the style of particular directors, getting to know some of the classic movie stars.

And I remember very well thinking to myself this would be a great field for me because I could almost reach back and touch the very earliest days of film. People like Cary Grant were still making movies when I was in middle school. Aside from people like James Dean, a lot of the people from the early days of film were still alive, and people from the silent era were just writing their memoirs and biographies.

So I thought, well this is great. This is an art where it's not like painting or music where you have to go back centuries. This is something where I could reach back and touch the beginning of it, really get my arms around it, and really understand it. So that was really when I began to think about film in a critical way. When you're 16, you're critical about everything anyway. And I, as a bossy oldest child in my family had a natural bent toward being critical so that worked well.

[Laughter]

Minow: But I think the most important and the most neglected part of being a film critic is that you're above all, a writer. If you don't write really well, clearly, evocatively, very, very specifically, vividly– if you can't do that then it doesn't matter how brilliant your insights are nobody is going to read what you write and certainly nobody is going to pay you for it. I had always wanted to be a writer as well. So, it seemed to me that all of that came together really well for me. I have a lot of opinions, I really like movies, and I love to write.

Kevin: I love it. So we're going to piggyback off of that and go into how did you find your voice as a critic? Because I know, for me, when I first started you know it was like I had my opinions but then at the same time I didn't necessarily have the confidence to…

Minow: Right.

Kevin: …to speak in my own voice. And then eventually, I was like, wait, let me just speak as myself. So, how did you find your own voice?

Minow: Well, that's exactly the right question to ask and that's really a two-part answer. Part one, one of the most important moments of my life was when I finally got a chance to write movie reviews for my high school newspaper, my senior year of high school. I turned in my first review and it had a lot of "kind of this and sort of that and could be this" and you know, very critical. My editor, who was just another senior at the school but who was more experienced in working at the school newspaper said to me, "Hey, if you're going to be a critic, that means you have to have opinions and you have to be willing to support them and advocate for them. That's what being a critic means."

And that was a real light bulb moment for me. You know, you're not really writing for the ages. You can change your mind. There are certainly films I've changed my mind about. But you if you can't write with a strong passionate point of view about what your response is to the film then you really should not be a critic. So that's part one.

Then I went to college. I wrote movie reviews for the college paper. Then I went to law school. I did other things for a long time. Sometimes I wrote about film but not on a regular basis. And then when the internet was invented, I was fascinated by it. I was on the internet so long ago that when I typed my name, people would write, "Are you a girl?"

[Laughter]

Minow: And it was really just a few college students, a few people in the military, and me. This is before the World Wide Web. This is back in the days of bulletin boards. So I was on the internet very early. I think I first got on in 1987 and I was very, very interested in it. And when the World Wide Web first began, I wanted to create a website, and at that time, I'm not only a lawyer but I was a mother of two young children. So every website that I had seen was basically here is our office coffee pot, here is my dorm room, here is my pet, here are my 10 favorite websites, there was really nothing happening.

And I said well, I don't want to write about my personal life. I am a grown up, I'm not in college . So I think I'm going to write some movie reviews. And then I had to really sit down and think to myself, who am I as a critic? Because the last time I'd written movie reviews I was in college. I said, well you know what, I'm the mother of young children. I think that that's something I can bring to the world. At that time we had video stores and you'd go rent videos and I would see parents looking panicked at the new releases shelf trying to figure out what was appropriate for their kids and what wasn't. And certainly, the teenagers behind the counter were not giving them any guidance on it.

[Laughter]

Minow: And I thought you know what? I can write movie reviews and I can bring what I am. I'm a woman. There are not that many women film critics. I'm a mom. There are not that many mom film critics. And being a lawyer and being married to an intellectual property lawyer, I got the trademark and the domain of movie mom. At that time, there were literally hundreds of websites, there were not even thousands of websites. So I got started very early, but those were the two steps. The first one was in high school turning in my first review and having my editor say "You know, take out all of this kind-of-sort-of-could-be language" . The second was going in as a critic as an adult and thinking about bringing everything I am as a person to what I had to say about the movies.

Kevin: That makes a lot of sense. I think what you're saying is basically knowing who you are and then speaking to that demographic in a sense, right?

Minow: Yeah. Well, I'm not speaking to that demographic because I'm not just interested in movie reviews by other moms.

Kevin: [Laughter] Right.

Minow: I'm interested in movie reviews by gay black men and a transwoman– those are actually people that I follow. I want to see everybody's point of view and I assume that my point of view is one that anybody could be interested in. Because again, it depends on how good a writer I am, and I'm a very good writer.

Kevin: All right. So, if it's true that there are only seven basic plots in the world, how do you keep a fresh eye for every movie that you see?

Minow: There are only seven basic plots. In my book I said thirteen but there are some overlaps there. Yeah, there are only seven basic plots, but that's been true going back to ancient Greece. And you know Oedipus is not just a story about a guy who kills his father and marries his mother. It's a story about the struggle to become who you are, to grow up, and to deal with terrible tragedy.

Those are all things that were true in ancient times, and they're true today. Whether it takes place at a high school or in an office or another planet, those are all stories that happen in our lives and that we want to understand. After all, that's the point of stories. They help us understand what's going on around us. They always say that the difference between movies and real life is that movies have to make sense. And that's what it is. It's helping us make sense of all the messiness and strangeness in our lives.

So there are seven plots. There's a plot of coming of age, there's a plot of going on a journey, there's of course, falling in love, all of those. And what makes them work or not work in a movie is how specific they are, how surprising they are. The plot is not going to be surprising but will it give you insight about that plot? Will it give you a new understanding of it? Will it give you characters to help illuminate that for you? And, so that's what you look for in a movie.

Kevin: All right. Nell, you're absolutely crushing this.

[Laughter]

Kevin: So, what advice do you have for the up and coming critic?

Minow: Well, I've got three pieces of advice to the up and

coming critic. I understand that there has been a debate just in the last few days on the internet about whether a movie critic has to understand film history. That's not a debate. The answer is yes, you have to understand film history. Now, everybody today is not as lucky as I was when I first started watching movies. Only, let me think – only 40 years after sound had come into movies. So, you know, I was lucky in that sense. But if you have not seen say the top 100 AFI American films of all time, if you are not familiar with the French New Wave, with Hong Kong films, with Italian neorealism, if you're not familiar with those then you do not have the palette to bring to whatever the latest blockbuster is at the multiplex. You don't have the framework. You don't have the understanding.

For example, this is the most trivial example imaginable but it just happened so I'm going to mention it. OK, so Fifty Shades Freed just came out last month, and it's a terrible movie. And I'm listening to review of it on a podcast and they're talking about how terrible it is and that's fine. Then they talk about a particularly terrible scene where Jamie Dornan sings the song Maybe I'm Amazed. It is terrible, that's one the greatest love songs of all time and he does a terrible job and it's a terrible choice. But OK, fine. So then it becomes clear as they're talking about it that they don't have a clue what the song is or where it's from or who wrote it, which is Paul McCartney. And that just took away so much from my ability to trust the rest of what they had to say about the film.

Same thing happened with a review of Million Dollar Baby that I read, where the critic didn't know where the title came from. You know, some of it you could do with a Google search but you have to know what it is you need to know. I think that if you don't understand what these things hark back to– I just saw a delightful movie called Lost in Paris that was a beautiful tribute to the work of Jacques Tati. If you didn't know about Jacques Tati then you couldn't really fully appreciate the film.

So number one is study film history, watch a lot of movies. Number two is read a lot of books. There are so many great books about directors, about actors– you know Ann Hornaday's book is good, they really help you understand. Then the third one is, as I said, you have to be an – not just a good writer, you have to be an excellent writer. You have to be as good a writer as you would have to be say, a novelist or to write magazine feature stories. Your writing has to be crisp. You have to have good adjectives, and you have to really be able to evoke what the film is about and have some insights to it. So be a very, very good writer.

Kevin: That is an incredible information, so valuable. One real quick question let's sneak in there. As a sub-question to this question: what advice would you have for female critics coming up in the game? Because I feel like in terms of like film criticism, it seems to me to be a male dominated industry. There are so many podcasts that are two white males that are talking about movies. But what advice would you have for female film critics trying to get their voice out there?

Minow: Well, I think in a way, the fact that there are so few, should open up more opportunities. I know certainly, Rotten Tomatoes is looking for more women and they're also looking for more politically conservative critics because you want to talk about a minority in the world of criticism. [Laughter]

Kevin: Yeah. [Laughter]

Minow: But we can talk about why that is some other time. But yeah, I think that what I would recommend is that there – the Alliance of Women Film Journalists, AWFJ is a fabulous group. I am so proud to be a part of it. Jennifer Merin, the founder of that group has been an incredible support and resource. So, there are places like that where you can find a sisterhood that will give you some feedback and some ideas.

Kevin: Awesome. All right, two more questions and we're done.

Minow: OK.

Kevin: Why is the film critic important?

Minow: I think film critics are important for three reasons. One is what I call, do I need an umbrella reason, which is, I'm looking at the newspaper, I want to go out tonight. Should I go to this movie or that movie? Sort of the yelp approach where you can just do a quick look. You don't have to read through the entire review because you don't want to spoil anything. But you get a quick guide on should I go to this movie or that movie? The second thing is, after you've seen the movie and I often recommend this to people, that's when you want to read the review to compare your reaction to the critic's reaction. You can see something you might have overlooked, to understand something that maybe you didn't understand.

And the third reason, and I think this is the most important one, is that I can just tell you right now Ready Player One is going to be a big hit. There's just nothing you can do to stop that from being a big hit. And that's fine. When a movie has got you know a multimillion dollar advertising budget and a best-selling book behind it, you don't need any help getting people to the theater. But where critics can really make the difference is in a small independent film that might be overlooked and that's where I think critics are really especially vital.

Kevin: Well said. Last question. Where do you see film criticism headed?

Minow: Well, you know when I was growing up, I was fortunate to be in Chicago when I was writing for my high school paper, where our local film critic was Roger Ebert. And so I had no problem getting access to his reviews because they came to my house and the newspaper every week. And then I went to college in New York and there was really no way for me to read his reviews anymore because the Chicago Sun-Times didn't come to New York. That's all changed now. You can read anybody you want from all over the world at any time you want and that's a wonderful, wonderful thing.

Furthermore, Roger Ebert was working for the Chicago Sun-Times and as long as he was going to work there, nobody else was going to get that job. Now, anybody who has an opinion can get their opinion out there and it's really survival of the fittest on the internet. You know, I remember many years ago, I came across a website from somebody who just started putting up movie reviews and I thought they were outstanding. And the next thing I knew she was starting to write movie reviews to the New York Times. She went from just sitting in her apartment writing reviews, somebody in the New York Times saw them and said, "I'm going to hire you." And now, she's a movie critic for Slate, and that's Dana Stevens.

So, there's this wonderful opportunity through the internet and through podcast for anybody who wants to do it, anybody who's willing to do the work, to get their voice out there. You know a lot of people say to me, “I’d like to be a movie critic” and what I say to them is, “OK, I just wave my magic wand now you’re a movie critic. Now comes the hard part, you have to actually write the reviews.” And when people say, I want to be a movie critic, what they mean is they want somebody to come and offer them a job to write reviews.

Well, I wrote about 500 reviews before anybody paid me. But that’s what I did. I wrote reviews for my own enjoyment for five years, from 1995 to 2000 and then Yahoo, which hadn’t even been invented when I started writing reviews called me on the phone and said “we want you to be our movie critic”. So, you have to be willing to do the work. But if you are, the opportunities are limitless.

When you say “I want to be a movie critic”, if you want to be a movie critic, write reviews. That’s all there is. Now, if instead what you want to be is a TV star, well that’s a different story and I have no idea how to tell you how to do that. But if you want to be a movie critic, the opportunities are there and all you have to do is be better than everybody else and then people will read it.

Kevin: Awesome. So just for clarity, do you think that basically, it doesn't matter what happens in terms of technology as long as we kind of go back to those three things that you talked about: knowing your film history, reading, and then being a great writer. If you do that, you can survive no matter what kind of changes and developments happen?

Minow: Absolutely. Yeah, absolutely.

Kevin: Sweet!

Minow: Yeah. And, you know, take the opportunities that

come to you based on what gives you the greatest audience, not on what gives you the greatest paycheck. Because if you want a paycheck, become a hedge fund manager.trans woman

Kevin: [Laughter] I love it.

CHAPTER 13

KENNETH R. MOREFIELD

Name: Kenneth R. Morefield

Medium: Online

Outlet: 1More Film Blog

Years active: 11

Top 3 movies: The Godfather, A Man Escaped, Rounders

Favorite Director: Luc and Jean-Pierre Dardenne

Kenneth Morefield is an Associate Professor of English at Campbell University in Buies Creek, NC. He is the editor of and a contributor to Faith and Spirituality in Masters of World Cinema (2008, Cambridge Scholars Publishing). Other works of note include his contributions to the anthologies: Perceptions of Religious Faith in the Work of Graham Greene (2001, Peter Lang) and The Deep End of South Park: Critical Essays on Television's Shocking Cartoon Series (2009, McFarland). He also maintains a collection of other film related writing at 1More Film Blog, his personal film blog.

Morefield has written numerous film reviews which have appeared in Christianity Today Movies, The Gospel Coalition, IMAGE Journal, WORLD, Christian Spotlight on Entertainment, The Matthew's House Project, Scope, Looking

Closer, and The Cary News. He is a member of the Southeastern Film Critics Association (SEFCA), the Online Film Critics Society (OFCS), a contributing critic to Indiewire and Rotten Tomatoes, and the founder of the North Carolina Film Critics Association (NCFCA). Ken also currently owns and administrates the popular Arts & Faith website.

Ken has always struck me as a deep thinker. I think that, as a man of faith, he is naturally more inclined to wrestle with the deeper questions as he did in Bible College (which he shares in our interview). When I think of deep thinkers, I think of a person who takes the time to analyze something. It takes care, patience, and a desire to find answers to whatever the topic is, in a way that isn't rash or found easily. These qualities come out tenfold in his writing. There's attention to details that one may gloss over and a sense of connection to the film in his reviews that goes beneath the surface of the film. You won't find those standards everywhere.

Kevin: First question, when did you first fall in love with film?

Morefield: When I first fell in love with film is a hard question to answer, sort of like the first time you fell in love with your wife. Some people have a specific moment and some people have an accumulation of interactions. I mentioned in the print interview that when I was in high school my parents took me to the old Key Theatre in Washington D.C. because they were doing a retrospective of five or six Alfred Hitchcock films that had never been released to the public before – after their initial offering.

That was a big deal at that time because in the early '80s we didn't have the wide selection of classic films on VHS – there were no DVDs back then. That was the first time I saw Rear Window, Vertigo, The Trouble with Harry, a lot of those classic Hitchcock films. I think that moment in Rear Window where Jimmy Stewart wakes up and he's got Grace Kelly leaning over him was somewhat intoxicating to a young American teenager. So, we'll call that a pivotal moment in terms of not just going to the movies at the local theater, but realizing that there was a whole world and history of the art form that I hadn't yet become aware of.

Kevin: What drew you to the art of film criticism? Because film critics take it one step further where it's not just barbershop talk about a film but actually breaking down films. So, what drew you to the art of film criticism?

Morefield: My academic training is in the study of literature. So I have a PhD in English and one of my field specialties was the history and practice of literary criticism. I think the first time it drew me to the art of film criticism then was a comparative genre analysis trying to think through ways in which a film is different from a book, a film is different from a screenplay, a screenplay is different from a book and so on. I was fairly late to get into the art of formal criticism looking at some of the actual filmic elements and I relied pretty heavily on examining them as narratives in the same way that one might examine the narrative of a novel or short story.

Certainly, there's a long history in film of literary adaptations, borrowing from other art forms whether they be songs or paintings or plays or books. I was really wanting to think about how those genres both stole from each other and revitalize or compliment each other.

Kevin: One of the things, for me starting out as a young

critic that I felt was a challenge was finding my voice. So, I wonder, how did you find your voice as a critic?

Morefield: [Laughter] Well, honestly, in terms of the question "How did I find my voice as a critic?", after I graduated from graduate school with my PhD, I spent four years in the Bible Belt, teaching at a very theologically and socially conservative Bible College. I think for me the process of finding my voice was really a process of thinking through and distinguishing what I believed about art and the world that art exhibited. Also finding the will or the integrity to be able to really say what is true rather than what you think the audience wants to hear.

I think that was a very fertile place or environment to sort of practice those decisions. I think whether you're working in a very fundamentalist environment, teaching there, going to school as a student, or just living there, you're confronted daily with that question of "Am I going to be conformed to the peer pressures overt and covert that really require me to sign off on what the latest orthodoxy is?". Not just orthodoxy in a religious sense. I mean cultural orthodoxy in terms of who are the right candidates, what are the right positions, what are the right views to take about social issues. I think you're confronted with those tensions daily.

To the extent that film exhibits the world around us, anytime you attempt to be true or introspective about what you're seeing, you're going to rub up against that issue that there are going to be people who read your stuff, who disagree vehemently with what the film artifact is saying about the world or what you're saying about the film artifact or the world. And they won't hesitate to let you know it.

So, I think really finding my voice was finding that way of being comfortable with realizing that there are going to be people who don't like what you have to say. As strange as it seems, there are actually people who read your stuff. A lot of times in this day and age, particularly with the internet, things just go out there and you can go through long periods where you don't get any response and you can lull yourself into thinking "Well, I'm writing for an audience of one – I'm writing for myself."

And then all of a sudden you write something or there'll be some sort of reaction and you realize, "Wow! This is actually out there in the world and someone is going to read this and not everyone will have the same view." So, I think finding my voice as a critic was learning to be comfortable saying what I knew to be true in spite of the fact that it wouldn't always be popular.

Kevin: I feel like that's great advice. And I want to add a follow-up question to that because I think that was one of the difficult parts for me. What you said about just being comfortable with going against the grain and kind of trusting your own thoughts and that is your voice, right.? So, the way that you grew up and your life experiences have created your personality. With so many voices out there, it's easy to jump on Rotten Tomatoes or see what someone else thinks and then let that influence you.

This will also go into the next question but keeping on the voice of a critic: how do you keep a blank slate to protect and guard your thoughts so that they don't get tainted? Does that make sense?

Morefield: It does. I don't assume to speak for you but I know you're African American. I am a Christian and I think both of us sort of participate as well in the broader marketplace of ideas, a universal marketplace of ideas and are also conscious of our voice within a particular community you know, a smaller community and why that's important.

Kevin: Mm-hmm.

Morefield: I'm reminded of Ta-Nehisi Coates during a keynote address at South by Southwest this year. He talked about coming to hate this sort of term "public intellectual" because he felt like anytime you find your voice as a writer or critic there's always people who want to co-opt that voice and use whatever success that you have had to advance their own agenda. Sometimes it's a good agenda and sometimes it's one that you agree with or are sympathetic with but that's not really your agenda.

I think in this age of Twitter and in pundits on shows and opinion pieces, it's very easy to become distracted and – I'm straying away a little bit from what Ta-Nehisi said – but also from getting away from just what your goal is to focus on what I've put the thought into, the research into and the work into and feel comfortable talking about to getting that co-opted into something that is more about being the mouthpiece for a particular cause and just spotting the same talking points that anyone else can talk about.

So that would segue into the second part of your question which is how do you keep the authentic voice while there is such a lot of chatter around you and a temptation to look up other responses. I would say first that it's not always illegitimate to look at what other people say. Sometimes the best commentary can be in the form of a dialogue, whether it's real or imaginary, between other people. Sometimes other people's thoughts, ideas or observations can trigger something in you where you're like, "Hey, there's something that's bothering me about that or there's something I like about that but I can't quite put my finger on it."

I'm not one of those critics that's just asking you to never read what someone else says until you've committed your thoughts down onto paper. Having said that, I think the easiest way to keep the authenticity of your voice is to try to read as little other criticism or responses about whatever you're writing about before you actually do it – try to limit that. Unless you have a particular purpose, like Ta-Nehisi said "you're actually researching a topic and want to be able to speak authoritatively about a topic".

There's a difference between speaking authoritatively about the responses to The Avengers, in which case you have to look at what other people are saying. Talking about The Avengers, you can say to yourself, "Well, I'm just trying to inform myself about what's out there" when really you're just fishing around for ideas or a hook because you're writing the umpteenth review about the umpteenth Marvel movie and have said everything that you really think could meaningfully be said about that particular genre or that particular idea.

Another way that I try to keep my voice fresh –and this is a little bit easier as some of the professional outlets that I write for had waxed and waned– but it took me awhile to realize I don't have to write a review for everything that I see. I'm not in that professional sort of model where someone is paying me to go see Deadpool 2 or Han Solo. And if I go see a movie and I have an idea then it's easier to run with it if I don't have a backlog of "Well I've got to do three or four reviews a week about a lot of stuff that I don't really care about."

I think in terms of younger people starting and keeping their voice, I would say be selective about what you devote your time to and what you write about. That can seem counterintuitive because at the beginning you're so hungry to get attention and you feel like the more I put out there, the more likely something could land in front of somebody's eyeballs. But I think the reality is that quality trumps quantity. You don't want– when someone finally does read something that you wrote –to have it be something that you did a half hearted effort on because you weren't really passionate or cared about whatever it was that was the subject of your time or your review.

Kevin: I think that was a great answer.

Morefield: Thank you.

Kevin: Yeah. This is the kind of stuff I wish I had back when I first started out. All right. So, the fourth question is – you kind of answered this already– if it's true that there are only seven basic plots in the world, how do you keep a fresh eye for every movie that you see?

Morefield: Well, I think I'll just pair it with what I had said on the written response, which is that I'm mostly a reader response critic. So, even if the plot is the same or it's similar, very rarely is a review about the plot. I don't think people watch or read reviews to get a sense of plot anymore. I think there are a few isolated parents who maybe read for plot because they want to decide whether or not to let kids go see the movies. But by and large, I don't think anyone's reading for plot.

My sense is – I don't have any data to back this up – the majority of people who read reviews, which seems to be diminishing on the whole are people who have already seen the movie and want to know whether or not they agree with you or you agree with them or are interested in some sort of take on that particular movie. So, I try to avoid plot summary and I don't necessarily have an issue with keeping it fresh if the plot is derivative. I will try to look at my own responses.

Sometimes if my response is a very stale response because I feel it's a stale regurgitated plot, then I might not write something. But if I don't respond in a typical way even though I recognize the sort of generic nature of the plot or the structure, then I might start examining my reaction and saying, "Well, what is it about this particular film that actually engaged me or that turned me off more so than other films that engage in the same tropes, style or plot action?"

Kevin: Awesome. What advice do you have just in general for the up and coming critic?

Morefield: Well, I've said in the written response – and my tongue was only half in cheek – figure out how you can pay your rent. I've been fortunate that I have full-time, tenured, teaching job that I could make a living off of. So, I'm not having to live on the edge of financial exigency. It's very hard to have principles or quality or selectivity when you know you're feeling that pressure of "I've got to beat the bushes" and finding something that will pay.

I think when a lot of people are starting out, particularly artists or writers, they sort of dream of that "Well, wouldn't it be great if I could make money doing this thing that I love and then it wouldn't be work?" And I think the reality is that even if you're doing something that you love whether it's teaching or writing or making film, it is going to be work. It is going to be hard. There are going to be days where you don't like it, you don't feel like doing it or you feel like doing something else. And I think that it's very hard to be principled. It's very hard to have to make a decision or a priority of the quality over quantity if you're beholden to the bottom line.

And I think certainly the financial reality – at least from people that I talked to – who are journalists either full or part-time or amateur is that the number of paying venues and the number of paying gigs are rapidly diminishing. I don't know that I think it's realistic for someone to expect like "Okay, I'm going to go into Communications or get an English degree at a liberal arts college, get a job at my local newspaper" that's just going to write three movie reviews a month and pay my mortgage. I think those days are gone – if they were ever there – except for a select few.

So, I would think intentionally about what you want to do and how you are going to do it. And if what you want to do is be a film journalist or write film reviews there's absolutely nothing wrong with that. I think that there are still niches or spaces for that but the "How am I going to do that?" increasingly incorporates the question of "How am I going to make a living while I'm doing that? How am I going to support that?" That makes some people uncomfortable because they feel like saying that the distinction between professional as someone who gets paid for doing it and amateur as someone who subsidizes their own work makes some people reluctant to get a job to pay the rent.

But the reality is, I think that's true in acting and I think that's true in teaching– we live in an increasingly global market or economy where more and more people are either doing more than one job or more than one thing. I think that you can work on your craft and hopefully still get paid occasionally while actually looking for other ways or opportunities that are going to make more money because I don't see a lot of film critics who are financially independent right now.

Kevin: That is a true statement. [Laughter] Two more questions. Why is the film critic important?

Morefield: I'm trying to decide how honest I want to be with this question. You know, I think in the last two years – maybe even beyond that, maybe even really with the last 10, 15 years and the rise of the internet – I think we've seen a general turn in culture away from critical analytical thinking toward punditry, toward opinion spouting and I think that makes people have a little bit more volatile in their opinions. I think it makes people oftentimes have a more casual relationship with the truth. I think that it makes people a little bit more focused on technique and how loudly, persuasively and often they can say something or get it repeated.

I think some criticism, like any criticism if it's done well, helps keep us honest and remind us that you need to start with – in formulating an opinion or response – the thing that's actually there, and call it "the film", "the truth", "the idea" or something like that. And then build your case around that. I think that there are more and more people who are just looking for films or books or ideas or talking points where they've already decided what they think about life and are just trying to riff on or retrofit an explanation or a rationale or a zinger or a talking point.

And I think as the internet or as journalism gets more loud and provocative and angry and repetitive, I think that really good analytical writing or criticism is so important both in terms of modeling critical thinking but also keeping people who are looking for that, and helping them to actually think through ideas and responses rather than trying to just persuade them to have my own.

Kevin: Awesome. Last question, where do you see film criticism headed?

Morefield: Well, again, the general consensus amongst the people I talk to, at least for the last 10 years, is "Oh, film criticism is dying." "Oh, Internet killed film criticism." And I think there's some truth to that. I think that there was initially some hope that the internet was going to be democratic and it has been. That it was going to take film criticism away from the 50 newspaper jobs or the 100 newspaper jobs and put it in the hands of a broader array of responses so that everyone could have a blog or a podcast. And I think we've certainly seen that.

But I think one of the responses to there being so many choices of just being inundated with so many different types of film criticism out there is that people have either stopped reading or stopped watching or stopped listening if it's a podcast. Or, [people] have become just very esoteric or familiar where [they say] "I'm going to listen to this podcast because I know this person or this is my friend" and you have this sort of micro conversations going on. I think those will always continue because people like talking about movies.

But certainly, the idea of the weekly review does seem to be on the out. I've had at least two publications that I know of that within the last five years said, "We're not going to write movie reviews anymore" or they may write the occasional critical piece or think piece but no one's clicking on that – no one reads movie reviews. I think then there's been some attempts in the blogosphere to say, "Well, I use the freedom without space restrictions or click requirements to do a lot more long-form criticism." And I think that certainly you know that's going to happen.

But I see some criticism sadly going the way of the book review – which I don't know that anyone reads book reviews anymore. I think that there will still be occasional critics here and there that are speaking to micro audiences, sufficiently smaller audiences. But I don't know that I will see a whole lot of influence in terms of the actual criticism on the audience or on the particular bottom line for a film. Studios now seem to be a little bit more interested in the aggregate rather than any one person's review like Rotten Tomatoes, Fresh Meat or the Metacritic sort of number. But again, that's a sort of conglomeration of a hundred different reviews. I don't know that I see any one particular voice emerging within that.

So that's a very pessimistic answer. If I've learned anything in 10 or 15 years, it's that things change very quickly and people who tend to be pessimistic like me will always extrapolate current trends, ad infinitum into the future. That future doesn't necessarily look bleak, but I think as we saw with the rise of the internet, things very rarely proceed in a linear progression the way that you think that they will based on the current moment.

So, you know that my head –the logical part of my head– says that film journalism and film criticism is diminishing and will continue to diminish and largely become irrelevant. My heart says art is important, people care about art. There will be you know — this may sound very Jurassic Park-ish – you know "Life will find a way", criticism will find a way. That criticism will evolve and survive and perhaps even go through renaissance periods of more topical or more relevance. How exactly that happens, I have no idea. [pause] But I hope it does!

CHAPTER 14

JOE NEUMAIER

Name: Joe Neumaier

Medium: Print, Radio

Outlet: 710 AM-WOR, MSNBC, Fox 5, Former Chief film critic and film editor at NY Daily News

Years active: 30

Top 3 movies: The Apartment, McCaid & Mrs. Miller, North By Northwest

Favorite Director: Billy Wilder

Joe Neumaier, host of the weekly "Movie Minute" on New York's 710 AM-WOR radio, has been a film journalist, critic, Q&A moderator, and radio/TV commentator for over 25 years. Formerly the chief film critic of The New York Daily News, his film writing has appeared in The New York Times, Time Magazine, and The London Observer, and his broadcast appearances include MSNBC, CNBC, CNN, New York's 77-WABC radio, and California's 1350AM-KSRO.

I met Joe after he moderated a panel event at the Annapolis Film Festival. At the time, I was just getting into film criticism and I had some questions. I had noticed how polished Joe was in moderating. He understood both the craft of filmmaking and how to control a conversation as a professional critic (which is an art form in itself) and I wanted to learn to establish such a connection with my own interviews. Before I knew it, he gave me some advice, his card, and he was off to the next event. I don't remember everything we spoke about, but I do remember how I felt upon leaving the conversation- it was a warm interaction. Really, this may speak to his character more than how I think film critics should interact with people, because I've seen it all. Making time to lock eyes with a person, to be present during that interaction, and to give back to up-and-coming talent is very important. It's something I try to make sure I do consistently these days. I think that's also why, outside of being good at his job, Joe has had a long career! It's these habits and behaviors that give me the impression he has a long a successful career ahead of him.

Kevin: So first question, when did you first fall in love with film?

Neumaier: I think like so many of us growing up in the '70s I've watched films on television. You know, I can still remember the logos of the ABC Sunday Night Movie and things like that. There was something about the form of watching a movie that, as a child of television, obviously growing up watching the Brady Bunch and Gilligan's Island and everything else, that really struck me as magical. The story telling aspect of film struck me. I fell into movies. I just dove in. I really found I liked the longer form.

I went to a lot of drive-in movies growing up in Milwaukee, Wisconsin with my family and there was something about seeing the films projected. There's only a few left around the country. I still try to seek them out. There's one called

Shankweiler's in Pennsylvania that I've been to, the oldest operating drive-in, still operating in the US since like 1934. It's off Highway 80 in Pennsylvania. So, I still seek out drive-ins because drive-ins are really where I found myself falling in love with movies.

I saw Jaws at a drive-in with my parents. I saw Grease. I saw Jaws 2. [Chuckle] I saw Disney films like One of Our Dinosaurs Are Missing and various other things. I saw Star Wars, of course, in the movie theater. So I saw movies in movie theaters, but going to a drive-in –8 which is funny because aesthetically we all sort of think about seeing a movie outdoors with that thing hooked on to your window where you can hear the sound and you're watching the screen through a window. You wouldn't think that that's the optimum place to fall in love with movies.

But when I was 7, 8, or 9 years old, it added to the sense of, I suppose, being transported. It helps make the experience of going to a movie something really special. And still I think kind of connects with me in a sense of coziness and family. Even if you're sort of sitting and watching a movie by yourself in a critic screening room or something I still love to do, which is to go in the middle of the day to a movie by myself for a regular screening. If you're alone with a crowd or if you're alone by yourself there's just something cozy about that experience. I think that I can relate that in some ways to falling in love with movies via the drive-in.

And so, obviously then as I got older and grew up with the cinema or with the movies of the late '70s, I would go to movies all the time in regular theaters as well. So interestingly, drive-ins growing up in the Midwest in the '70s was my gateway drug.

Kevin: What drew you to the art of film criticism?

Because I think it's one thing to just watch movies, fall in love, but you know to actually speak on what movies are, what drew you to the art of film criticism?

Neumaier: As I got older and was in high school and college, I would of course read Pauline Kael and Dwight Macdonald and James Agee and so many of the classic film critics. But that's only important film critics. But when I was 12, 13, and 14 years old, watching Siskel and Ebert on the local PBS station first in Sneak Previews and then what was Siskel & Ebert's At The Movies. Originally, when they were at PBS, I watched them from the very beginning. Once that show was syndicated, because growing up in Milwaukee, they were in Chicago, I loved their film reviews and the way they discussed films. Their enthusiasm for films wasn't tempered by their intellectual dissection of film and I saw that they could co-exist. And so, you could think about films in a discerning way and maybe even have some problems with films you love or love films that really have big structural flaws. So, watching them in the late '70s, and then reading the local film critic in Milwaukee then, it was Doug Armstrong in the Milwaukee Journal. I would read his film reviews every Friday. So reading those smart critics and when I got older I would read the Sun Times or the Tribune to read Siskel or Ebert in print because newspapers were on sale in Milwaukee.

It was a great entrée into the machinations of a film review and a film critic's mind. To use that great Fitzgerald quote of "the sign of a first-rate intelligence is you can hold two competing notions in your head at the same time" kind of thing. I sort of thought about film criticism that way where it wasn't just rave reviews about things and sometimes complete pans.

But the things that drew me were those gray areas, the complexity, and the way that film was spoken of as an art, and as an important topic to chew on and converse with people about. I wrote my first film review at 14, but that made me think there's more going on here than sort of the entertainment value that sitting and watching the 1966 Batman movie, The Flim-Flam Man, or Planet of the Apes on TV. Then you sort of say, "Well, what's going on with those movies? What do I like? What don't I like? Why do I like these things?"

And so, as a young person growing up watching Siskel and Ebert, reading Doug Armstrong in the Milwaukee Journal and then just being aware of the culture of criticism in general – music criticism, theater criticism and then film criticism specifically – that drew me in. That notion that you can love things with flaws and you can find flaws in the things that you love. You can take them apart and see why they work. Why does the cinematography work this way? What purpose is the cinematography proving? How is the music emphasizing one emotional note or the other? Is this a great screenplay with a weak director? Is it a weak screenplay that a great director makes better? All of those things.

I still love that! I still love taking films apart in that way. Even just for fun saying, you know, "Here's why that works." "Here's why that resonates with me." And then the other aspect of that which we can get into in subsequent questions but, is the personal note. I've always avoided using the first person in my reviews because I feel like your byline is already there. You're lucky enough and honored enough to be able to put your opinion out there in the world.

Within that context is like you're discussing with someone

your personal response to a piece of art and film is the most populous of arts. To quote Ray Bradbury, the purpose of life is to kind of go inside someone's head and look out at the world through their eyes and say, "Oh, that's how you see things."

It's reading film reviews that you're able to see how this particular writer, how he or she saw this film. And maybe you connect with it. Maybe you understand something a little bit differently from reading in the review. Maybe you understand why you didn't respond to something. Maybe you realize something about the film itself, the making of it, or at least the emotional connection filtered through this person's own personal opinion. I think that that's a really resonant thing for me and always has been since I started reading reviews and watching Siskel and Ebert when I was like 12 or 13.

Kevin: All right. How do you do you find your voice as a critic? I definitely think that you know, [Laughter] when you're first getting into the industry, you can look to the greats like you said, but especially these days there are so many people that are commenting on film. So, how did you find your voice?

Neumaier: Yeah. I was lucky enough to go to a high school in Milwaukee that had a school newspaper. My freshman year of high school in 1982 in September or October I went to them and said, "I would like to write film reviews" because I loved writing. I was writing stories and writing things down and I would write– I guess what now you would call fan section about Star Trek or Planet of the Apes or something silly, or Twilight Zone. So, I would write these stories but then I also decide to combine my love of film with my love of writing.

I briefly wanted to be a veterinarian, but I thought that seems like too much work and too much blood. Little did I know that film criticism would also have work and blood in it. But I went to them and I went to the teacher adviser and I said I would like to review film. And so, my first film review was in October of 1982 for Richard Benjamin's My Favorite Year. I still have the review here in a pile of stuff from high school. It's in a nice album that I have. And I give it a good review, positive review. I liked it. I still like it. It's got problems but I still like it.

In fact, later on, I was lucky enough to interview Peter O'Toole, for I think it was Troy or something when I was at the New York Daily News. At one point I asked him a final question at the end of the half hour and he sort of unfolded himself, his full six foot three frame or whatever, from this chair. He was aged at that time but still sprightly and fun and sparky. He was wearing like a lime green suit and he draped his arm around my shoulders and ignored my question I asked him and said, "All right Joe I'll give you one more."

He walked me to the door and he told me some anecdote about being in the RADA in the '50s. And it was sort of my own personal, My Favorite Year moment which is very funny. And really [Chuckle] meant a lot to me.

So, I started writing, my freshman year of high school, and I wrote three or four reviews a month throughout high school. Then I started writing again when I got to college at the University of Wisconsin in Milwaukee. I wrote for anything that I could, school – one of the two schools, the college newspapers that were there as well as two or three independent newspapers around in the '80s in Milwaukee. One called WAM, and then one called The Shepherd Express. Then I would do radio reviews for a jazz radio station, and I started writing for the AM daily paper the Milwaukee Sentinel.

Throughout all of that, including in high school, maybe especially in high school, I got a sense of my voice as a critic. I got a sense of writing for an audience and writing for myself in a way and trying to find the middle line between those two. When you're young or even when you're not so young, it's not always easy to find that. But, I was able to find a way into myself, my persona as a writer that I find the most pure, for all the different types of writing I may still do, including for broadcast, or for consulting. I still find that all of it comes from the experience, the training that you have as a critic, as a young writer.

Winnowing down ideas, organizing that structure, telling a little story about a film, the film experience, what you thought of it, what works with it, having all of those choices that you have as a writer be in the service of having a conversation with the audience about this art, or this artist if you're talking about, the director or screenwriter. And so it kind of comes from this conversational tone but also being – as I said, being honored to be in the position where you have a platform to write about it.

In high school, people used to always, you know friends of mine used to say, "Oh, yeah, well who are you to say?" And I think all of us a critics have always sort of dealt with somebody who tells us that you know. [Laughter] And in high school, of all places, you're both the boldest you'll ever be probably and the stupidest you'll ever be. And it was sort of funny to be able to have that response of "Well, you know, I'm somebody who has been watching movies for a long time. I'm reading about films all the time." I had tons of film books all through high school. And you're kind of coming to it as a – maybe not necessarily a scholar but certainly who's perhaps read, or studied in arts, enough to make you feel that you have something to share.

So finding that voice through my reviews was really critical and crucial, and continues on. And of course, it's always evolving. You're never really fully done, I think as a writer, you know you have a voice, a consistent voice, but I think that sometimes that voice can be adjusted. Sometimes it's adjusted depending on now, in the freelance world, who you're writing for, and who that audience is.

I think that kind of comes off more when you are revisiting a film. If you're writing about a film that you loved for a long time or a filmmaker, you can sort of reassess. I think that reading things you've written about, one particular film or one particular filmmaker that maybe you wrote about 20 years ago or 10 years ago and then writing of them now, just as much as they may have changed or your opinion may have changed, your voice changes just a little bit too. It's always consistent but it's also always changing, if that makes sense.

Kevin: If it's true that there are 7 basic plots in the world, how do you keep a fresh eye for every movie you see?

Neumaier: Yeah, that's a terrific question. And I think that you almost have to go into every movie like you would when you were so young single person going to every date. [Laughter] It's like every, every movie, every film deserves its own fresh take. It's own fresh place in your mind and in your heart. And if you go into a Marvel movie saying, "I hate superhero movies" you are not going to be open to the – some of the extraordinary circumstance – some of the extraordinary moment in those movies.

If you say, "I don't like this particular genre or this particular actor" you are going to miss out perhaps on seeing them anew or watching them change. I don't know how I do it but I think maybe it's just a frame of mind. You need to be able look at them as if you are seeing a movie for the first time. Because you are seeing that movie for the first time and your experience of it should be as pure as you can be without seeing. Every time you go in, you're not always going to be like that, but the goal is to try, I think, to try and make it as fresh as you can.

Kevin: Awesome. All right. What advice do you have for the up and coming film critic?

Neumaier: I would say I have two bits of advice. One is to watch as much as you can. I used to work in a video store and I feel I think that helped in my education of being a film critic. I worked in a couple of video stores in high school. I'd bring things home and stay up all night with buddies and watch stuff that we rented and – going to movies all the time.

So now, with all the terrific streaming services, as much as I miss video stores, there is no reason to not be [cinematically] educated. There is more opportunity to have that at the click of a button than ever before. So, watch as much as you can. Give yourself a little film festival, say, I'm going to watch a Krzysztof Kieslowski film festival or I'm going to give myself a lesson in Truffaut and watch Truffaut films of the '60s or whatever.

See as much as you can and then also read as much as you can, obviously, because great readers make great writers. Read film criticism from James Agee in the 1930s and '40s onward. And some of it might seem clunky, some it might feel dated to read Bosley Crowther in The New York Times. It's a whole different experience. But it's important to read the film criticism from the historical point of view and then contemporary film criticism as well, which is also a terrific burgeoning point of so much criticism out there. Read what you can, get yourself informed, and see what other people are saying and how they're saying it.

Kevin: Perfect. Why is the film critic important? I think on the flip side you could say, you know, is the film critic important?

[Laughter]

Neumaier: Yeah, right. You know it's funny. I think readers who sometimes– and at the Daily News I got this a lot – people who would say, "I like what I like and I don't care what a film critic says." Every critic has gotten that response in the public sphere at some point, whether it's at a dinner party or a response online or somebody writing into the newspaper or whatever. Somebody is going to say, "I like what I like and I don't care what critics say." or the – or the corollary of that which is, "Oh, if you like it I know I won't so I don't go see it." Or "if you say you don't like something I know I will so I definitely go." So, there are always those responses.

I think the reason why the film critic is important is because it keeps film, again that most populous of art forms, it keeps film vibrant and it keeps it in the conversation and makes film something to talk about. We all love talking about movies at gatherings. You're on a picnic on the fourth of July and somebody brings up the latest blockbuster, we're all going to have opinions. If you've seen it, or even if you haven't seen it, you're all going to have opinions on it. You know, "Oh, I like that actor. I like that actress. I don't like that type of movie. That kind of thing scares me. This kind of thing is not exciting." We all have opinions on movies.

And so, when you're reading an opinion of a critic, I think what makes a film critic important is that you are privy to a master class, in a way, in conversational movie going, in learning why somebody who studied it, somebody who's thought about it – is giving their opinion. You may not always agree. But just like going to any other expert for things, if you're listening to an expert opinion, you may not ultimately agree with them, but to hear what they have to say, how they have to say it, ties film in to all the other arts and all the other things that make a culture vibrant and evolving and exciting.

And also, that most populous and congenial of things, which is we're sitting around the dinner table and saying, "Did anyone see this movie?" and we all respond. It's sort of the bridge between academia and the dinner party or the dinner table. It helps us find the commonality in all of this art, some of these arts, some of it high art, some of it low, but all of it worthy of attention. And I think film criticism makes all films worthy of attention.

Kevin: Last question, where do you see film criticism headed?

Neumaier: You know it's tricky. I think that – or maybe it's not so tricky. I think another thing we often hear is the refrain of everyone's a critic. And now of course, with the internet, everyone sort of can be a critic. [Laughter] But I think that's a good thing for film criticism in general, because it makes it a less rarefied position and makes it open for more diverse voices. That said, I think that you do have to be discerning, and I think discerning is sort of maybe the key word when you talk about where film criticism headed. Just like if you are reading a food critic talk about a restaurant, that is different from reading the comments on Yelp. One person has got a slightly elevated palette and another person is just a person who's going to have a dinner. And what did they think? Both of them valid, both of them valued, and both of them should be listened to. But, you have to be able to discern the level of experience, the level of study that's gone into this response. And the respect that I think they're giving to the reader. I think that that focus is maybe headed to a place where it's not oversaturated but it's perhaps under-curated you know.? And I think that maybe there will be websites, and Rotten Tomatoes does this, obviously Metacritic and things like that, where you can go and check out these critics.

Now, maybe there needs to be another site for critics who are not affiliated with major newspapers or something or major radio stations or whatever the case may be, so that they also have a curated space. And some of those critics may go on to be the critics that we talked about and the critics that are vital. All of the critics groups today and at the time that we are speaking right now, you would think that there's an attrition but in fact, they are burgeoning it. I think that they're flowering in really a great way, which speaks to the excitement that young writers have and the opportunities they have out there via the internet and other sources to let their opinions be known.

You could maybe say that perhaps the best thing that's coming out of it is that diversity of voices. That we have more women voices coming, more minority voices. Everyone is kind of coming to the party now in a way that thirty years ago, they wouldn't have been able to. And that is perhaps the most crucial thing that the future of film criticism is headed towards, which is a much more democratic with a small D, egalitarian and diverse room full of voices

CHAPTER 15

DESSON THOMSON

Name: Desson Thomson

Medium: Online

Outlet: MPAA, The Washington Post

Years active: 21

Top 3 movies: Rules of The Game, Singing In The Rain, Wayne's World

Favorite Director: Nicholas Ray

Desson Thomson writes speeches for Charles H. Rivkin, chairman and CEO of the Motion Picture Association of America. Thomson grew up in England, moving to the United States at 17. He attended American University, graduating with a degree in visual communications and cinema studies. He worked for 25 years at The Washington Post, starting out as a feature writer for the Style section before transitioning into other categories, where he eventually had his longest tenure as the one of the newspaper's longest-serving movie critics. After leaving the Post, he reinvented himself as a speechwriter in the administration of President Barack Obama. He has worked as a speechwriter for the U.S. ambassador to the United Kingdom, as well as with the Policy Planning Office of the U.S. Department of State as a speechwriter for Secretary of State Hillary Clinton, an undersecretary of state and the secretary of commerce. A communicator on many levels, Thomson is also a longtime singer and songwriter, as well as a screenwriter and a fiction writer.

I met Desson as Professor Thomson at American University. He was my Film Criticism professor and it was in his class that a fire sparked within me. After watching Modern Times, hearing him breakdown the film and realizing there was so much more to it than what I thought I understood, I was hooked on formal film criticism. From there, I watched film after film and heard many of his breakdowns, allowed me to see a different side of the medium I loved. Desson isn't a verbose critic. He's to the point and slices into the heart of what's going on in a scene and a movie. Thus, he's a memorable voice in film criticism!

Kevin: When did you first fall in love with film?

Thomson: I fell in love with film definitely when I was 8. My father took me to see Lawrence of Arabia. And he told me that if I fidgeted, he was going to put me out in the lobby while he watched the rest of the movie. I walked in terrified and I didn't fidget once! I realized that I loved movies and I wanted either to be in them or talk about them or something. I knew that they had to be in my life somehow.

Kevin: What drew you to the art of film criticism? What made you go from the little boy that didn't fidget and loved movies to actually writing about movies?

Thomson: Well, what I loved about film criticism was the knowledge that everybody loves movies and I was able to engage a lot of different people into what it is that captivated all of us. That was a wonderful opportunity to have that chance to talk to all of us collectively about the one thing we all love.

Kevin: How did you find your voice as a critic? Because I think that's one of the most difficult things for me when I was getting into film criticism is with all the voices that flood the internet now, making sure that you just speak in your own authentic voice. So how did you do that?

Thomson: The first thing I learned to do was to believe in my voice and that there was some value to it. And the fact that I had gone to film school at least gave me some authority to talk about the movies. But the most important thing was your personal point of view got to be amplified. And so, I believe that the responsibility of a good film critic is as much to assess the movie as it is to give the audience the benefit of his or her full-blooded voice.

Kevin: If it's true that there are only 7 basic plots in the world, how did you keep a fresh eye for every movie that you saw?

Thomson: Well, I think even the most cynical and jaded film reviewers go in with new hope to a movie. And in the same way that music only has 8 notes to it, every song is different. So we go to a movie knowing that while there might be some similarity to plot, it's the way it was done, it's the particularity of the movie.

So, I was always looking for something unusual and you can always – you can almost always find it. And as I went through many, many years, I actually started to enjoy the movies that I hated the most because it just gave me a chance to talk to the audience about other things that were far more interesting.

Kevin: So if I can just expanding on that, because I think

that is an interesting thing when you talk about a film that you don't necessarily like. But when you said that you were able to talk about something that's a little far more interesting, can you just extrapolate upon that a little bit more?

Thomson: Sure.

Kevin: What were some of the things that you did?

Thomson: Well, for instance, when I went to see Jackass 2, I just – I could have thought to myself, "Is there someone who can shoot me in the head?" or I watched it and I suddenly looked at it in other ways and I thought to myself, "This is really about young people testing themselves and this is something that is going on through history. The young man always wants to test himself and in very silly ways."

And so I thought, "What would someone like Joseph Campbell think about Jackass 2?" And so that became a far more interesting thing for me to think about than to actually go, "Gee, I like the way he stuck a knife through his leg or whatever it was." So it just became a deeper conversation.

Kevin: That makes a lot of sense. But that's also a good tip because yeah, sometimes it is hard to write about those movies that will be easy just to say that it sucks or it's childish, et cetera.

Thomson: Yeah.

Kevin: So, what advice do you have for the up and coming critic?

Thomson: First of all, just loving the movies is not enough. I would say that you need to have a life and you need to think about things that are bigger than the movies because everything is big and movies are about life so you don't just review the movie, you review the life what it's about too. So you need to have – the more breath you have in your brain, instead of just thinking about, "Gosh! Two movies ago, the hero wore a red cape, now it's a blue one." I mean you're just – you should go to nerd hell.

But I think I don't ever want to read those reviews because that's just a tiny little rabbit hole. But you can make it a big, huge expanse of experience if you look at life – you look at movies in the context of life is really what I'm trying to get to.

Kevin: Why is the film critic important? And I think on the flip-side, you could say, is the film critic important or relevant?

Thomson: I have to say I don't read film reviews very much because most film reviews don't talk about things that I really care about. I don't really care about the specifics of the movie. I'm going to watch the movie and enjoy the specifics on my own. What I care about is the way they look not just to that movie but the way they look at life, the way they express themselves, the things they have to say.

So, a good film critic should also be able to be a good architectural critic or a good food critic. So, I look for people who are transcendentally more interesting than the movie they are reviewing.

Kevin: Interesting. So what you're saying is that the person that doesn't just look at it for entertainment or just the movie itself but brings in more than just what's on the page in terms of analysis.

Thomson: It's infinitely more interesting to me. I mean yes, there obviously is a market for consumer film reviews but as soon as that movie ends, do you ever want to read that review ever again for the rest of your life?

I want to read a review over and over again and say, "Boy! The way you wrote about," name a movie from the past that no longer matters, it's 20 years ago, "but what you said at the time was so interesting." It just remains interesting.

So to me, that's the difference between a great critic and a critic.

Kevin: Awesome. All right. Last question is where do you see film criticism heading?

Thomson: Well, more and more people are talking about everything on the internet in a banal way but also in an interesting way. So there's a lot of space for this to get ever greater because expressiveness is really the thing that I think one of the things that makes us different from animals. Animals don't sit around campfires and tell stories or talk about things. So that's what – that is our responsibility to develop and make into an ever-increasingly larger art form.

CHAPTER 16

SUSAN WLOSZCZYNA

Name: Susan Wloszczyna

Medium: Print, Online

Outlet: USA Today, Washington Post, RogerEbert.com, The Credit and more

Years active: 17

Top 3 movies: Mary Poppins, any Billy Wilder film, any Hitchcock film

Favorite Director: Alfred Hitchcock and Billy Wilder

Susan Wloszczyna spent much of her nearly 30 years at USA TODAY as a senior entertainment reporter working her dream job: Visiting the New Zealand film set of "The Lord of the Rings," being a zombie extra in George Romero's "Land of the Dead" and interviewing countless show biz figures including icons (Vincent Price, Shirley Temple, Peter O'Toole, Mr. Rogers), A-list stars (George Clooney, Julia Roberts, Meryl Streep, Will Smith, Denzel Washington) and big-name filmmakers (Steven Spielberg, George Lucas, Martin Scorsese, Jane Campion, Nancy Meyers, and more).

Wloszczyna's positions at the newspaper included being a film reviewer for twelve years, as well as working on the Life section as copy desk chief. Now, unchained, from the grind of daily journalism, she views the world of movies with fresh eyes and a new perspective. Susan is a storyteller at heart, which is something that becomes a strength of hers in her criticisms. One of my fondest memories is having lunch with her and Jason Fraley between films at the Middleburg Film Festival, and listening to her talk about her experiences in the industry. You can tell when someone is a genuine fan of movies, living out a dream of talking with the people they grew up watching, because regardless of the trials that may come with the job, they still see the silver lining and have an appreciation for doing it. I think the critics that never lose that wonder and excitement do a great job of infusing those qualities into their writing! Susan certainly does.

Kevin: All right, Susan. So, the first question is when did you first fall in love with film?

Wloszczyna: Well, I was lucky to have my dad because he was my portal into loving movies. A large part of my parent's courtship entailed going to film because back then there wasn't anything like TV or streaming or anything like that. If you went on a date, chances are you went to a movie. I was born in 1955 so I grew in the '50s and '60s and I was greatly affected by Disney in a big way.

I think the first movie I saw when I was three years old and that was Sleeping Beauty. What affected me was not so much the princess part of it, but I just remember seeing when the Maleficent put a curse on the roses and they grew these horrible gnarly thorns and he had to cut his way through that. That scared me because I thought roses were nice – [laughter] my because my grandparents had them in the backyard. That kind of magic had an effect on me.

Again with Disney, I adored Mary Poppins. For me, that was my Star Wars. I loved Hayley Mills. The other thing my dad and I shared more than Hayley Mills and Disney stuff was Shirley Temple films, which were always on TV back then when I was growing up. So, I think part of it was that I was innately drawn to female characters as well. I thought, "Look at her, she's just great, you know? I could be that."

[Laughter]

Of course, I took tap dancing lessons and things like that. I enjoyed the whole thing – she's an orphan and yet she's being herself and being lovable and everything that got her to reach out to the world and be accepted and all that. There was something about that fantasy that got to me. The other thing is, back then TV because you didn't have to buy a film channel – I mean there were a lot more movies on TV, older ones. When you're a kid, you have no concept of "These people are from 30 years ago or 20 years ago" or something.

Kevin: Right.

Wloszczyna: You just kind of go for it. I remember the first movie that scared me when I was a kid was Abbott and Costello Meet Frankenstein, because it's supposed to be a funny movie. But I never saw a Dracula portrayed before or the wolf man or any of those things that are in that film. That was my introduction to horror and it freaked me out – these bats flying around and everything. [Laughter]

The other image I saw was the silent movie Nosferatu, which I ended up covering Willem Dafoe bringing that to life. That guy is horrible – almost insect-like features just creep me out. For some reason, I thought he lived down the street from my grandmother because I saw the movie in her living room.

[Laughter]

I had a very active imagination and that I think helped me engage with movies in a very personal way that maybe more sane people didn't have. But the cool thing was: later I got to interview Shirley Temple when she got her Kennedy Center Honor. Hayley Mills came to D.C. with The King and I at the Kennedy Center and I got to talk to her. Unfortunately, this was only on the phone, but Julie Andrews when she did the Princess Diaries – that was her return to Disney after many, many years so I got to talk to her for that. What I love is that my job got to make my dreams come true and meet my idols, which I was rarely disappointed – except for George Clooney but that's a whole other story. [Laughter] No, he turns out to be nice.

Kevin: All right.

Wloszczyna: I was pretty young – I was three when I figured out what was what. Also, I was nuts for the Mickey Mouse Club and all that stuff. So it pains me very much now that Disney has become this money making machine where everything is re-made and it's all sequels and origin stories and cartoons are made live action and vice versa. It's all these sequels and they aren't really making a whole lot that's new. There's Coco and things like Inside Out, but those are rarities now.

Back then, they created this whole genre of family entertainment that is still there but nobody puts as much effort into it as they did back when they were first starting out.

Kevin: Yeah.

Wloszczyna: That kind of depresses me, but I still love covering musicals and that's partly because of Shirley Temple and animation. Those were two genres I really glommed onto in a big way when they were coming back in the '90s for animation and then musicals came back with Chicago and Moulin Rouge! as well. That made me happy.

[Laughter]

So, sometimes it pays off.

Kevin: So, what drew you to the art of film criticism? I know you say you went for a stint of just reviewing but what drew you to the art of it?

Wloszczyna: The art of it. Well, I think I was always drawn to newspapers. In Buffalo there were two – right now, there's only the Buffalo News but they had the Courier-Express. They devoted – they both had movie reviewers on staff. Again, I was always obsessing about movies and going to them. I made a list in my head when they started rating films, of the mature ones I couldn't see. [Laughter] I go, "I'm going to watch them when I'm old enough." Some kids want to drink or drive a car. Me, I wanted to watch the adult movies. [Laughter]

I think I always had opinions, I never was shy about sharing them. I just realized from reading the reviewers in the local papers that I could actually maybe do this. On TV, there were celebrity critics like Rex Reed and Judith Crist and Gene Siskel, and of course, later on Siskel and Ebert and Pauline Kale. They would go on talk shows and talk with Dick Cavett or whoever, Merv Griffin, and they were treated like celebrities. So, it seemed to me, "This is kind of cool that you can just spout off about what you think and then people think you're great."

[Laughter]

But I also like thinking about movies. I do think I have come to realize one of the reasons I love the Oscars show so much – again, my portal to that was Mary Poppins when that was nominated because it was finally a kid's movie that I had seen and I was wishing that it would win all of the awards and everything. I think people look at what's won through the years and they criticize them for being awful movies or whatever. But for me, for example, in 2005 when Crash won over Brokeback Mountain, I think it said something about society – that the voters couldn't go for Brokeback Mountain for some reason but they did for Crash, which no one talks about [Laughter] anymore, you know?

Kevin: Right.

Wloszczyna: For me, I was always into the Oscars which was tied into all the stuff. I think as far as the art of film criticism, I don't think I considered it art back when I was just in grade school or something. But I will say that anytime there was a school paper I could write for, I would try to write reviews. In fact, when I started at USA Today, I started out being a copy editor. And then because I have opinions and I talk, I got put in charge of the Life Section copy desk for four years – which almost killed me. But then one of the critics – who was a woman – left. They had two critics all the time. I tried to try out for that and the first movie I did as a review was Honey, I Shrunk the Kids, which was right up my alley.

They had other guys up for it and the main critic, Mike Clark, was a middle-aged man. I said, "You know, why wouldn't you want another woman? Why would you want two middle-aged men with the same voice looking at the same movies?" And it didn't even dawn on them that maybe that was a good point – and it was. I'm glad they saw that because that got me my job for doing that. So, that was great.

I always wrote things beyond being in charge of the copy desk because the thing is, when you're at place and they slot you into being one thing– like the copy editor chief – then you get typecast that way. I think showing them – I did a column for their weekly magazine for Sunday editions in their local papers called USA Weekend. For a while I did a video column for them – for free – and that way I showed I had more in the vault than just yelling at people and meeting deadlines. [Laughter]

Kevin: Right. Right.

Wloszczyna: But as far as film [criticism] being an art, it took a long time for me to develop that. At USA Today – I write for Washington Post now and very often they give me far less space than RogerEbert.com, my main outlet and that's how I got into freelancing after leaving USA Today in 2013. For them, they want more thoughtful insights, right? Not just a plot summary and a few funny lines and then you're out of there. I had to really change the way I thought because I would have, at the most, 12 inches or something to write for USA Today because they liked things brief and tight and witty and all that stuff. I had to change how I do it.

When I write for Washington Post, they want that too but they want a little more depth – but in a smaller space. [Laughter] It's funny because my friend works at the Kansas City Star and she was using the reviews I had and she said, "I really like your reviews because other places go on and on and you're more concise, yet you say the same things in the tight space." So even online, you have to keep yourself reined in a bit. I think when I read something that goes on and on – that's the art. To make a statement and back it up and do all the things that you have to do in a tight space, I think is an art as much as writing [Laughter] a thousand words.

Kevin: Exactly. That makes sense. I also like what you said about the fact that you spoke beyond just what you are doing and getting assigned. One question that I wanted to ask is: how did you find your voice as a critic? Because I think sometimes when I first start, we look around or now you can check Rotten Tomatoes to see what everybody else is saying. But how did you find your unique voice?

Wloszczyna: Well, it depends on the review. I was the secondary film critic for the longest time, and Mike Clark would assign me things. It actually was a good thing to happen, but I kept getting things like every Arnold Schwarzenegger film – and I mean before, not just The Terminator, but other things that maybe weren't quite so great. And Steven Seagal – I did every Steven Seagal film. The one thing I noticed is in every movie he does, he trashes a restaurant or bar or something. I mean it's weird but it's true [Laughter] if you go back and look at his films, it would be there.

Kevin: Yeah.

Wloszczyna: And then also, Jean-Claude Van Damme. I got all those things. I remember one thing I hated was Predator. There was a sequel and Arnold wasn't in it, it was Danny Glover. [Laughter] And it wasn't quite the same because he's not Arnold Schwarzenegger. Not that he's not a good actor, but I'm like, "I mean, really?" It was eye-opening.

The other thing I did was – I saw a lot of movies I would

never see on my own and pay money. It tells you – you think you're watching a bad film but really it's not as bad as the stuff I was subjected to sometimes. I remember seeing a Steven Seagal film about the oil industry – something ground– and Michael Cane was in it and Steven Seagal – it was his directing debut so it didn't screen for critics so I had to go to the first showing, wherever I went. There were a lot of guys there but by the end, he was making the speech at the end to make a statement about how drilling oil can hurt the environment and all that – I was the only one left at the end. [Laughter]

I will tell you the movie that got me out of film criticism, because I saw a bunch of really bad films in a row in 2001, like Say It Isn't So, Saving Silverman, nobody knows these films – Bingo which was a stupid dog movie. Then I saw Freddy Got Fingered – that was the one with Tom Green from MTV back then.

He had his little cult of guys and he was weird and obnoxious and all that stuff and they were all into it, right? It was such a horrid movie that again, little by little at this free screening, guys were leaving. Again, I ended up being amongst four other people who probably fell asleep during the show. That movie just put me over the edge because I realized, like I said, they were appreciating my other work. All the screenings back then were basically at night. I just couldn't keep up with both parts of my job so I made the choice, and they were glad I did. So, there was somebody willing to be the film critic as well with Mike.

I had enough. [Laughter] But now, I'm glad I do what I do and I gladly do any film. It's easier now with links as well. We didn't have that choice back then.

Kevin: Well, I think you were probably getting to it – but

in terms of how you found your voice – like with Steven Seagal, you'd noticed that he would always destroy a restaurant and then you started to write about that, right? So that kind of became something that you did.

Wloszczyna: Well, I actually interviewed him. I would see some and I felt like a specialist so I interviewed him. And almost the same with Jean-Claude Van Damme, I just became an expert. What it did – to see things that were out of my comfort zone just made me more informed about what movies really are. You can't just see arthouse films or Shirley Temple films or whatever. You really have to know what's going on because I don't think you could be as informed as you should be if you're going to make statements and back them up in reviews.

You have to do some research before you see a film sometimes as well – I think that helps. You can't just sit there and soak it in and then think you're informed on what you saw. That's true with interviews too. I do a lot of research before I talk to people so I don't embarrass myself.

Kevin: All right. So, if it's true that there are only seven basic plots in the world, how do you keep a fresh eye for every movie you see? Because even with what you just said after seeing a slew of Steven Seagal films, you still have to write about it. So, how do you keep a fresh eye coming into each film you see?

Wloszczyna: Well, I don't know how I keep a fresh eye because I'm older than you and my eye isn't going to be as fresh as you anyway. [Laughter] I think it's hard not to come in with assumptions when it's a filmmaker you like, so you know what they're capable of, you're going to have assumptions anyway. I don't know if I could be actually without assumptions. So if they defy those assumptions, if they're bad or meet those assumptions or more if they're good, then that's fine.

But I think what I most rely on is: given the type of film it is, if it's a comedy, it should make you laugh, right? Some comedies don't because they're dark or they're weird or like punch-drunk love I still don't get and I don't need to get. I don't have to like every Adam Sandler film or whatever. But I did laugh at Happy Gilmore, so I gave it a pretty good review.

And a thriller should thrill. If it's supposed to be a tearjerker like Terms of Endearment, it better make me cry at some point. A musical should make you go out humming if you can. A mystery should keep you guessing. A horror movie must be frightening a little bit. Sci-Fi – I expect to see something maybe I've never seen before. A biopic should somehow fill you in with some things and some facts about the subject and get closer to what that person was like.

I think they might be the same plot because they have to meet certain expectations or what genre it is. But I like when they have their way with it, that it's different. That Phantom Thread – I still don't know what to make of – I don't know what genre they are. Did you see that?

Kevin: No. I missed it.

Wloszczyna: It's one of these movies that I was intrigued by but I didn't love it, but then I didn't quite know what he was after and it just didn't fit any – I don't think it's one of the seven basic plots.

[Laughter]

Because it's sort of a love story but it's sort of about this megalomaniac dress designer. As for Thomas Anderson films, he usually uses a lot of people in his movies and this was very tight and intimate – almost claustrophobic for him – because this designer didn't get out much beyond going out to breakfast and eating a lot of British foods. [Laughter]

There are movies that surprise you but I couldn't quite flat that. There are a couple of movies this year for actors that broke the mold and had people guessing. Three Billboards left people not knowing what to think about it and some people were upset by it, others loved it.

It's actually not so bad to have divisive film that's seen by a lot of people – I mean one reason I don't like superhero films is because I've been covering them since the first Spiderman with Toby Maguire. To me, they're almost always the same plot.

I think one thing that Black Panther did – it was very different from what we're used to and that was a good thing. Basically, they're all just saving the world and fighting each other and it gets very boring me to see a whole lot of special effects [Laughter] because I like reality. I think sometimes you can tell the actors aren't invested in green screens.

I think after a while you lose the essence of really being physically in a place like that – even with the best actors. But they're also using all our best actors and hiring and putting them in indie films and I was like,"Can't they make real movies? Why do you have these long-term contracts?" I mean it's just Robert Downey, Jr. – I think all he does are these movies. It's a shame because I think he's much better than these films allow him to be – and now I'm getting off the subject again.

Kevin: [laughter] It's ok. So, to the point of what you just

said – when you go to a superhero film, we expect that there's going to be a villain, and it's kind of like the whole Joseph Campbell thing where there's a reluctant hero and then they go into and then it seems like – I think the question is in terms of how you have to write about it. We could easily just say, "Well, you guys know what happened basically, you know there was a fight and the good guys won" or whatever. But how do you say "Okay, I'm going to approach this and tell what happened" but without making it redundant? It's still original and unique when you're writing it.

Wloszczyna: Yeah. For example, I'm going to talk to Jeff Goldblum this week for Isle of Dogs and I decided I needed to finally see the Thor: Ragnarok movie, and he got a lot of good press about it. I also like Flight of the Conchords and that New Zealand director who did Hunt for the Wilderpeople. So I said, "OK, I'm going to watch this. I'll give myself the two hours or whatever it takes to do this."

I didn't review it, but even though it did break some conventions and it made fun of the conventions and things like that, I still wanted it to be better than I thought it was. And I thought Jeff Goldblum was very funny doing his Jeff Goldblum things. But again, I'd just rather watch [Laughter] a movie – not that it has to be old people but I love British actors and I love British films and I love Maggie Smith and I love Judi Dench. I love them all because of the things I grew up with – I lived in Buffalo, near Canada, and there were all these British films that weren't on American TV.

I always love seeing Allen Bates or Albert Reed or Tom Courtney, so I'm very much prejudiced to more realistic films. I like films more when they show life. But if I'm assigned to a fantasy like Beauty and Beast, I sometimes have to get out of my head. For example, I saw the new Cinderella with Lily James and it seemed pretty by the book and all that. But then I was thinking that she's so innately good and her good is her super power, right? She didn't become vindictive and fight back and take up a sword or something. She was just very sweet and kind and that was her defense against all the evil in the world.

The more I thought about what Kenneth Branagh did with that, I realized I had a young daughter and if this was the first movie she saw, I would be very happy with this. Sometimes movies aren't made for me but I get assigned them and then I have to honestly talk about them, but I shouldn't deride it from the get go. I should open my mind a little bit – you just teach yourself to grow up a bit and see it through other people's eyes too and what the audience is for. Does that make sense?

Kevin: Yeah that totally makes sense. I get it.

Wloszczyna: I gave it three stars, I didn't love it but I did appreciate it for what it was. I think it was to its benefit that it didn't go the snarky, making-fun-of-everything route. Sometimes sincerity works. [Laughter]

Kevin: Right. Exactly. Yeah. Like you said, sometimes it's like – I am a huge fan of The Fast and the Furious but those things are in no way Oscar worthy films. It's just fun to me. So, I understand finding that balance.

All right, only three more questions. One is what advice do you have for the up-and-coming critic or film reviewer?

Wloszczyna: For me, whatever contacts you have, don't ever burn your bridges. That's the one thing that has taught me to survive in the freelance jungle, which I'm glad I left in 2013 because it's only gotten more crowded with other work. Critics used to work for mainstream media and were losing their jobs and things like that. Every day I find someone who's no longer doing what they're doing.

But if you maintain your reputation, you don't burn bridges, you are a good doobie – you have to not be afraid to ask. The reason why I ended up being a freelancer – I only do one review a month usually for Washington Post but they pay a lot. I get a paper and plus they have a network where they send the reviews out to all sorts of papers around the country who can afford a film critic. I'm in all sorts of places. [Laughter] Not that I got paid more for that exposure but it can't be bad.

Renee from PR Collaborative told me, "You know, you should really ask Michael if he needs help because he seems to be overwhelmed." I never thought to ask Michael Sullivan – in fact, he writes for the Washington Post – but I did and it turned out to be very easy for me because I don't think of myself as this veteran critic with all this stuff. I think I'm starting over still, so I don't think "maybe they think I know something". [Laughter] And also, you meet your deadlines, you don't make more work for them, you don't ask for things you shouldn't – I'm very grateful for any place that will have me.

As far as up-and-coming critics, I don't know. I'm glad I didn't want to be this [Laughter] because I started at USA Today thirty years ago and before that I worked at the Niagara Gazette for four years. I became the Feature Editor before I left and joined USA Today. But again, I always did more than I was asked. That's something too, because I wrote reviews for them, I wrote restaurant reviews for them, and art gallery reviews for them.

There was that Shaw Festival in Niagara-on-the-Lake which was nearby. I reviewed plays because I wanted to be a reviewer and the only way you can learn how to do that is to get your voice and learn how to judge something and let other people know why you think that is by doing it. [Laughter] I was lucky because I started thinking that way when I was very young and grew into it. I don't know if people still say "I want to grow up to be a movie reviewer".

Kevin: I doubt people do. But I think that at the same time, with technology these days, there are children that say "I want to be a YouTuber".

Wloszczyna: Oh, and they do it.

Kevin: Yeah, exactly.

Wloszczyna: There's other ways to do it and get an audience. If you have a personality, go with it. I don't know if I did back then. [Laughter] No one wanted to hear me talking when I was 12.

Kevin: I think that's most parents – like, "Can you please go over there a little bit?"

Another question is: why is the film critic important? Do you think that we serve any purpose as film critics?

Wloszczyna: I do, because I think each decade since the advent of film in the early 20th century, it has revealed our attitude as a world and as a nation. It reveals what people thought was important.

That's why I love to cover the Oscars because I've kind of been a cinematic sociologist. For example, there was a book that I reviewed about High Noon and how the screenwriter for that was in the blacklist of studios during McCarthyism and all the anti-communist scares and stuff. And for a short period, before all that was even a thing he registered as a communist but now you would say that and people would laugh.

[Laughter] I think it explained one thing that was always a mystery to people: how the movie, The Greatest Show on Earth, about the Ringling Brothers circus and was directed by the guy who did The Ten Commandments. What was his name? [Laughter]

Kevin: Cecil B. DeMille?

Wloszczyna: There you go. As a kid, there was this whole state of circus movies when I was growing up and I loved them so I had no problem with that movie. It's corny as hell, okay? Besides that, I don't think it's the worst winner ever but some people do. But the reason why that won – Gary Cooper won for best actor and then the music won. But it won nothing else and it's still considered one of the biggest mistakes made by Oscar votes but it was only because it represented what that time was like and how scary it was. People took their lives because of it because they couldn't make a living.

I think if people read that [book], and it'll tell you something about how movies can really affect what goes on in the world. To shut a writer like that up – he did get rescued like the way Trumbo did if you saw that movie.

Movies aren't just movies, they are like little portals into what people were thinking at that time. If you look at all the musicals that were out in the '60s, I think that's something about the way people looked at life. But then things were sneaking in that were showing that a change was coming, like 2001: A Space

Odyssey or Easy Rider and things like that. My favorite era of movies was the '70s because they made adult films that kids could see, and that's what I wanted. I remember seeing a double bill of Bullitt and Bonnie and Clyde when I was a teenager and that was such an eye-opener for me and that was just two movies.

It opened my world to see movies, not that they're not imagined places – even if they're set in reality obviously things are changed. One of the reasons I like films with women in them, especially ones who were older than me, is that I was able to try on the lives they were leading on screen for size and see how it felt and learn what it was like to be a human being and a woman in a world like what we were growing up in.

The '70s to me is the richest period of moviemaking because of the topics it handled and how it was presented in a very adult way. Now, I don't think our movies are all that adult. I think escapism is fine – there is nothing wrong with that – but I think money is all and I think that's why streaming is great.

Unfortunately, there is so much out there now that as a society it's very hard to rally around one film like Black Panther or Wonder Woman or Avatar or Titanic. Those things where we all come together because everybody seems to like the same things – it doesn't happen anymore and I think that's why the ratings for the Oscars is so low this year because it's not that they're bad films, it's that people don't have the communal thing about "Oh, did you see this shit? You have to go see it. And Black Panther is unusual." That happens far less than it used to back when there were fewer choices of what to watch.

Kevin: This is a great opportunity to piggyback on what you just said as the final question which is: where do you see

film criticism heading? Obviously like you were saying before, you've seen it where things went from print and then to digital and online and all that. Now, as you've said, we're at a point where you can stream movies from your house. You don't have to go out to the theater. So, where do you see film criticism headed?

Wloszczyna: Well, I think I have a set of people where I trust their opinions. There's this guy, Bilge Ebiri, who was at New York Magazine for a while and he's now at The Village Voice which is only online – it just stopped being a print paper. There's this guy Steve Whitty who worked for the New Jersey paper and I kind of trust him. Guy Lodge who writes for Variety now, I liked him. You find people you'll follow. But as far as the countless people that do it for very low pay but they diligently do that – it's a lot of the same opinion [Laughter].

But I'd rather do a small film and come in and tell people, "Hey, don't overlook this just because there's 8,000 commercials everyday for the Avengers or whatever." And I think I always like finding those little arthouse films that were special over the obvious that all you have to see is this kind of stuff, a sequel to something you already saw or read or a remake. I like alerting people to new things and I like people who do that for me.

I am more attracted to people who are willing to do the work for me and tell me "You need to see this film." I think if people really want to broaden and use film right, they can seek out things that broaden their horizons. You want to a mix of friends, you don't want people echoing what you know already in order to feel that you truly are a well rounded person.

I know it's too easy to just do the things you like and get the wrap. The first time this happened to me was with The Sopranos where I was more excited to see that week's latest episodes that I was to review any movie I was seeing. That was right around the Freddy Got Fingered time. [Laughter] And I just said something is happening because things on TV are getting much, much better, and it's kind of continued that way. There are shows where I'd rather binge watch than go see the latest whatever.

I think comedy is the category that is really hurting. I don't want to blame Judd Apatow but I think now with all these R-rated films it's not clever anymore, [Laughter] as much as it used to be. Things happened and times change and you got to do what you got to do to make money. You can't stop technology, you can't stop innovation, but sometimes it's not always a good thing to have countless choices.

So, I do think critics are important for that. I don't know where it's going but I'm just glad I'm still able to do it. At some point, I'm going to say, "Screw this, I don't want to do this every week anymore." It's like a blank slate every time and you have to think of a way to do it – it's never easy. I mean I'd rather do an interview because I have all my material. I just have to think of the questions. When you're writing about movies, you have a blank slate in your head, for the most part. But you know that. [Laughter]

ABOUT THE AUTHOR

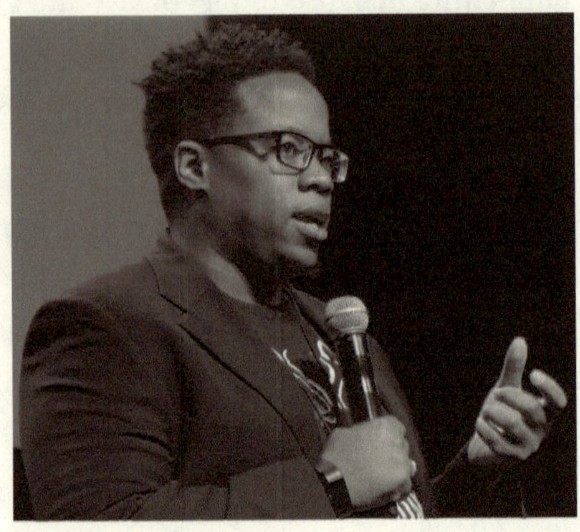

Kevin Sampson is not just a lover of movies, but a practitioner in raising new, diverse voices in the craft. He is a member of the Critics Choice Association, Washington DC Area Film Critics Association, North Carolina Film Critics Association, and African American Film Critics Association. His reviews and podcast can be found on his site www.picturelockshow.com. He is the founder/director of the DC Black Film Festival and principal of Picture Lock PR, a boutique PR firm that represents some of the many great independent films he sees on a regular basis. He received the 2018 Donald H. McGannon Award for his work with women and people of color in media. He has sat on the board of the Film Festival Alliance since 2019.

Kevin is the author of Army of One: PR & Marketing For The Indie Filmmaker and accompanying online course PR For

The Indie Filmmaker.

Born in Orangeburg, SC, he currently resides in Charlotte, NC with his wife and two children.

www.iamkevinsampson.com

www.ingramcontent.com/pod-product-compliance
Lightning Source LLC
LaVergne TN
LVHW091130080826
845145LV00008B/2106

* 9 7 8 0 5 7 8 7 4 9 1 2 9 *